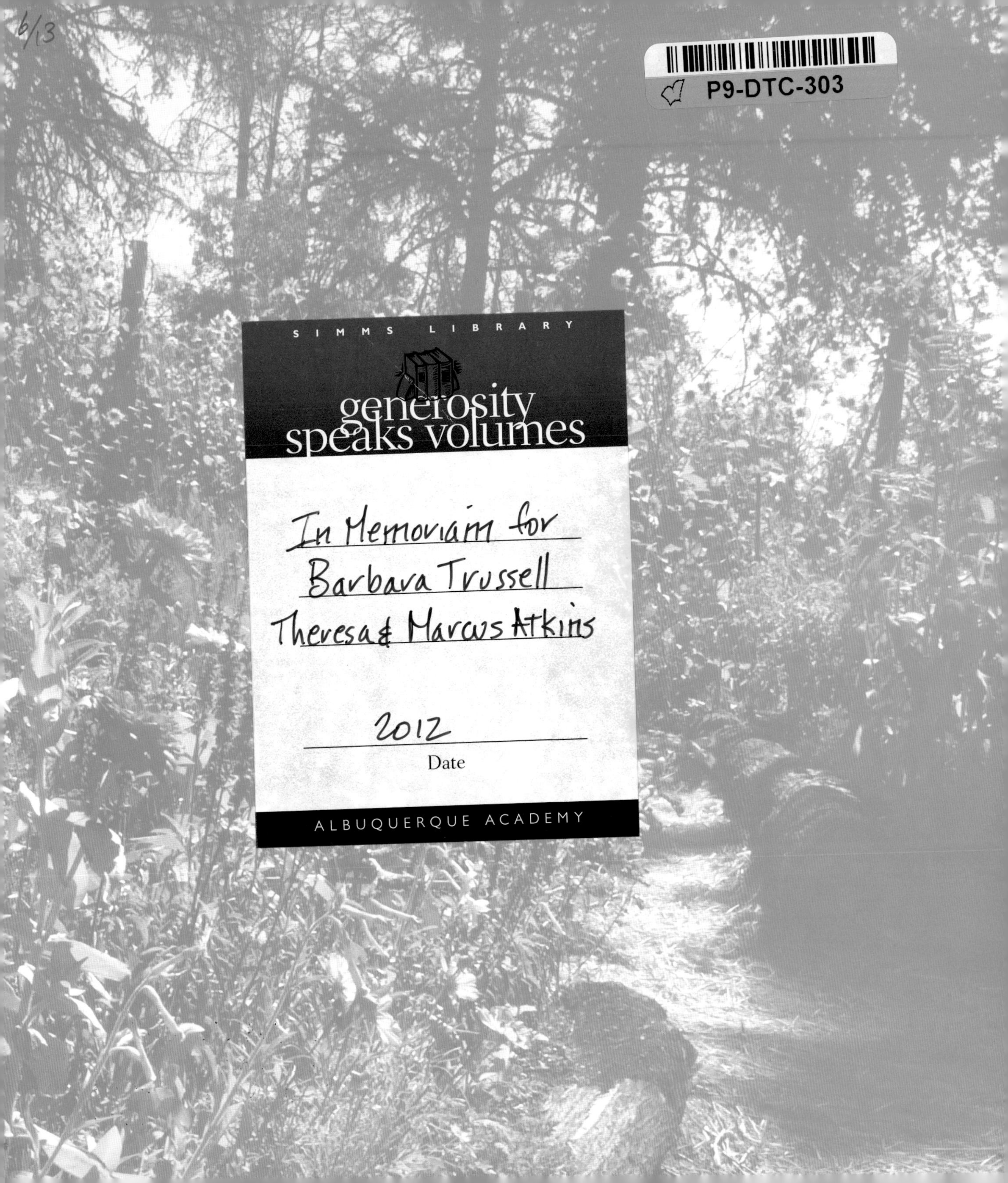

The
ARTIST
the
COOK
and the
GARDENER

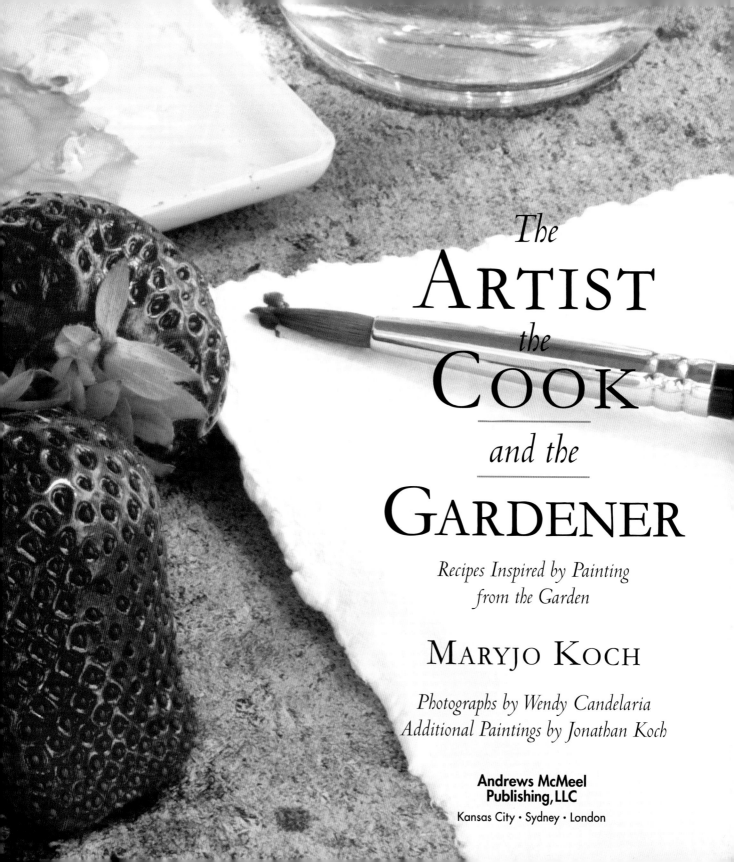

The
ARTIST
the
COOK
and the
GARDENER

*Recipes Inspired by Painting
from the Garden*

MARYJO KOCH

Photographs by Wendy Candelaria
Additional Paintings by Jonathan Koch

**Andrews McMeel
Publishing, LLC**

Kansas City • Sydney • London

GALERIE BEAUBOURG
CHATEAU NOTRE-DAME DES FLEURS
06140 VENCE

Produced and designed by Jennifer Barry Design, Fairfax, California
Production Assistance: Kristen Hall
Developmental Editor: Eve Lynch

13 14 15 16 17 SDB 10 9 8 7 6 5 4 3 2 1

ISBN: 978-1-4494-2146-5

Library of Congress Control Number: 2012939287
www.andrewsmcmeel.com

Attention: Schools and Businesses

Andrews McMeel books are available at quantity discounts with
bulk purchase for educational, business, or sales promotional use.
For information, please write to:
Special Sales Department, Andrews McMeel Publishing, LLC,
1130 Walnut Street, Kansas City, Missouri 64106.

Contents

Foreword   9

Introduction   11

Soups   19

The Winter Garden   43

Salads   45

The Spring Garden   63

Sandwiches, Pizzas & Savory Tarts   89

The Summer Garden   117

Sweets   123

The Fall Garden   147

Basics   150

Acknowledgments   153

Resources   154

Index   156

FOREWORD

ver the years I've taken many of Maryjo's classes. I think of each one as a wonderful mini-vacation. I remember the excitement of driving up the beautiful California coast to the little town of Bonny Doon, entering Maryjo's wooded driveway bordered by a charming white picket gate, and rounding the corner by her lush flower and vegetable garden to the barn where she has her studio.

Upon entering her studio, the first thing you notice is the long painting table laden with the painting subjects of the day. Roses, shells, miniature forests in enamel containers— one for each student. The studio walls are lined with high shelves like a magnificent natural history museum. Maryjo's extensive library of art and nature books is accompanied by boxes and bottles containing all kinds of specimens collected from nature—eggs, birds' nests, shells, insects, rocks, and pressed botanicals.

I've enjoyed the Painting Leafy Greens class, the Fruit and Flower classes, every class— and the lunches! Maryjo's table is set with lovely tapestry napkins and rustic tableware. Every meal I've had in class was memorable. Her soups and salads are extraordinary! There is an attention to detail and flavor that comes from Maryjo's three passions: painting, cooking, and gardening. She has an artist's eye for the perfect culinary balance in her menus and on each plate. Her meals are what I consider to be the new definition of a tearoom lunch—with a contemporary California sensibility. Maryjo's fare is satisfying and flavorful yet at the same time delightfully ethereal.

You are in for a real treat with this book. Visually, it's both stunning and inspiring, but I think you'll also find it to be a practical guide to cooking just the way we want to eat today. Enjoy!

—Gayle Ortiz, author of The Village Baker's Wife

INTRODUCTION

Just like a meal stimulates our senses and nourishes our bodies, the garden nourishes our spirits. Our mind's focus on petty problems is pushed aside and is no match for the pondering of miracles found in a garden. The fragrances, hues, shapes, textures, and sounds that emerge from tiny seeds are miraculous and mesmerizing. Walk into a garden and all five senses are aroused: from the fragrance and color of a flower, to the sounds of birds and wind, to the taste of freshly picked produce, to the feeling of moisture in the air or the soft leaves of lamb's ears and the prickly thorns of a rose. Think of how walking into your favorite restaurant appeals to your senses and elicits an appetite; so too can walking into a garden. Some gardens are like a gourmet meal, offering the perfect balance of color, scent, form, texture, sound, and taste.

Gardens have been an important part of my life since I was very young. I grew up watching and exploring the gardens my parents created. In my 30s my parents gave me a parcel of their land to call my own, and I was challenged to create my own garden. Because of that challenge I studied landscape design. As my garden grew, I became fascinated with the wildlife that visited and made homes there, especially birds. I became interested in ornithology and began studying and painting the birds' nests that I found. It wasn't long before friends and family discovered my fascination with nests and began sending me what they found in their own gardens.

11

I began selling my paintings and developed a line of birds' nest note cards that I sold to gift stores such as Smith and Hawken and The Nature Company. It was in Smith and Hawken that my first book producer discovered my work and came up with an idea for a book. Our first book project, Bird Egg Feather Nest, *was hatched, and we went on to create three more books for a nature series. As my books became popular, I did a number of book signings for the California Academy of Sciences in San Francisco and I was eventually invited to teach painting at the Academy and at the Monterey Bay Aquarium. I found that I enjoyed teaching painting and decided to offer weekend classes in my home near Santa Cruz, California. I have since created a studio to accommodate my many students, who come from all over the United States.*

My experience with teaching over the past 15 years has helped me to develop a method in which to learn to paint using subjects found in the garden. Beans, seeds, eggs, leaves, fruit, flowers, and sand are excellent subjects to start with. These are all prerequisites to my more advanced

Nothing is more completely the child of art than a garden.

SIR WALTER SCOTT

OPPOSITE, LEFT, AND ABOVE: Scenes from a spring flower painting class at my studio and garden; students arrive in the morning and go out to the garden to select their flower bouquets to paint. My studio shelves are lined with an array of treasures from nature—shells, nests, insects, pinecones, and dried botanical specimens. When the weather is warm, we break for lunch and eat *al fresco*; at the end of the day we have a class critique and discuss our work.

painting classes on subjects such as birds' nests, eggs, insects, and shells. The garden provides the subjects of our paintings and at the same time nourishes the spirit. Many of my students have remarked that they feel rejuvenated after class, as if they have been to a spa!

My classes typically begin in the morning and last until the late afternoon, with a midday break for lunch. When I first started teaching, students would bring their own lunches. I noticed this caused the class to become divided at lunchtime, as students would break off into several small groups to eat around the studio. To bring the focus of the group back together, I began creating a casual lunch, serving it family style at a large table outdoors, weather permitting. Over time, I developed a delicious repertoire of recipes using seasonal fruits, vegetables, and flowers freshly harvested from our garden. It was only a matter of time before I took our garden-inspired meals one step further and began using the painting subject of the day in my lunch recipes. Learning to paint flowers became Flower Petal Salad; painting figs became Fresh Fig and Black Forest Ham Sandwiches.

13

A garden is a delight to the eye and a solace for the soul.

—SAADI

ABOVE AND RIGHT: My garden provides a colorful selection of blossoms for my flower painting classes. Flowers such as borage, roses, calendula, and nasturtiums also provide petals for our Flower Petal Salad, which I serve the class for lunch.

The social interaction and occasion to meet new people is a fun and important part of my classes. Gathering at lunch makes for interesting and lively conversation. It also provides a much-needed break from the serious work of painting. The break provides rest for the eyes and mind as well as nourishment. My departure from class to prepare lunch is also well planned, as I have found that when I am absent, students tend to push themselves to paint on their own without my hands-on assistance.

Throughout the year my classes are scheduled to coincide with what's in season in our garden. Leaf painting class is usually in spring. One of my favorite painting subjects, birds' eggs, also inspires my spring classes. I like to serve Spring Asparagus Frittata with Peas and Peppers (page 113), using fresh farm eggs and asparagus and peas harvested that day from the garden. Flower painting is scheduled for early summer when the garden is ablaze with color. We pick our flower subjects to paint, and for lunch I serve a lovely Flower Petal Salad (page 61). The Painting Fruits and Berries classes are held in midsummer, while Painting Seeds and Pods is held in late summer when beans are harvested. For that class I like to serve Toasted Sourdough Crostini Topped with White Bean Purée and Sautéed Greens (page 99).

ABOVE AND LEFT: A sign mounted on a rare Santa Cruz cypress tree guides students to the studio. Nature and gifts from the garden inspire my painting as well as my cooking. Class lunches are often soups, salads, and sandwiches made with seasonal garden ingredients. I grow what we love to paint *and* to eat.

I use my garden to grow visually interesting vegetables, fruits, and flowers, in varieties one may not find in grocery stores or even at a farmers market. I am also very fortunate to live near a Mecca of small farms. The world-class restaurants of the San Francisco Bay Area demand excellent and unusual produce. I am able to purchase heirloom tomato seedlings from one of my favorite local farms, Love Apple Farm, which also provides vegetables for the Michelin-starred restaurant Manresa in nearby Los Gatos. Anyone who has tasted home-grown tomatoes would concur that their flavor is far superior to store-bought tomatoes, but their beautiful colors, irregular shapes, and vines also make more interesting painting subjects. The recipe for Silky Tomato Gazpacho (page 26) is heavenly during the peak of our late-summer tomato season. Similarly, borage flowers are so simple to grow but are not something typically found at the florist or grocer. However, the flower's extraordinary form and color are perfect for learning to paint, and it's also edible! I use the beautiful blue borage flowers in my salads and also press them into rounds of goat cheese.

When I plan my meals, visual interest plays an important role, along with what is available and what is seasonal, and of course the meal must also satisfy my hungry students. The meal must also be able to be partially prepared in advance of class and ready for heating and plating at noon. I hope this collection of recipes inspired by painting from the garden will nourish your own creativity as it has mine, whether it's in the kitchen, at the easel, or in the garden!

—*Maryjo Koch, Bonny Doon, California*

Soups

Fresh Pea Soup with Mint and Crème Fraîche   21

Carrot Soup with Chives   25

Silky Tomato Gazpacho   26

Cucumber-Avocado Soup   29

Zucchini Blossom Soup   31

Summer Squash and Fresh Corn Chowder   32

Chicken Vegetable Soup with Pasta Shells   35

Minestrone with Rosemary-Garlic Oil   36

Butternut Squash-Apple Soup   39

Creamy Mushroom Soup Topped with
    Sautéed Shiitakes   40

Peas are one of the first vegetables that we enjoy in spring. I love watching them grow, attaching their delicate tendrils to my garden trellis as they climb. Painting botanicals of pea plants is fun; I use my liner brushes to capture those thin, curling tendrils as they twist and turn. This soup is delicious served hot or cold. When the weather is warm, I like to serve the soup chilled in little teacups as a savory aperitif. As an extra benefit, the solids left after straining the soup make an excellent dip when mixed with plain yogurt and spices and served with pita chips.

4 tablespoons unsalted butter

1 cup minced shallots (from 5 large shallots)

3 cups chicken stock

4½ cups shelled fresh peas or thawed frozen peas
    (if frozen, from 2 18-ounce bags of peas)

1 small head of butter lettuce, leaves separated

2 cups loosely packed fresh mint leaves,
    plus 8 small sprigs for garnish

1 cup crème fraîche

Fine sea salt

Freshly ground black pepper

Pea leaves and tendrils for garnish

1 Melt butter in a large saucepan over low heat until foaming. Add shallots, cover, and cook, stirring occasionally, until tender and translucent, about 10 minutes. Meanwhile, bring chicken stock to a boil in a medium saucepan. Reduce heat to medium-low and add the peas, lettuce, and cooked shallots to the simmering broth. Cover and cook until peas are tender, about 5 minutes. Add mint, cover, and simmer for 5 minutes longer.

2 Working in batches, puree the soup in a blender until smooth. Strain the soup through a fine-mesh strainer into a clean saucepan; discard or reserve the solids. Stir in the crème fraîche. Simmer briefly, about 3 minutes. Season to taste with salt and pepper and serve immediately, garnished with the reserved sprigs of mint and the pea leaves and tendrils. If serving cold, let the soup cool and then transfer to a bowl and chill, covered with plastic wrap, for at least 2 hours before serving.

RIGHT AND BELOW: Peas and bok choy are two of my favorite vegetables, and they do well in the cool winter climate of Bonny Doon. I have a netted garden trellis for the peas and they climb as they grow until ready to harvest in early spring.

I love mint and cook with it a lot. I grow several different varieties and enjoy the varied flavors they impart. I use fresh mint in soups and for herbal tea; sprinkle it on salads, pizzas, and tarts; and garnish desserts with leaves and bright green sprigs. Its refreshing taste and aroma enliven every dish.

As for the garden of mint, the very smell of it alone recovers and refreshes our spirits, as the taste stirs our appetite . . . —PLINY THE ELDER

Spearmint

Lavender Mint

Corsican Mint

Pennyroyal

Candy Mint

Pineapple Mint

Egyptian Mint

The best

English Mint

CARROT SOUP WITH CHIVES

The changing colors of each season often inspire what I like to cook. This silky, sweet carrot soup is a dish I like to make using fresh carrots from the garden in early autumn. The bright orange color resembles the changing leaves of our ripening persimmon trees and garden pumpkins.

2 tablespoons butter

1 medium yellow onion, chopped

⅓ cup dry white wine

1½ pounds carrots, peeled and thinly sliced

2 cups chicken broth

⅛ teaspoon ground white pepper

Pinch of ground nutmeg

1¼ cups whole milk

2 teaspoons minced fresh chives

An artist cannot talk about his art any more than a plant can discuss horticulture. —JEAN COCTEAU

1 Heat the butter in a large saucepan over medium heat. Add the onions and sauté 5 minutes until softened. Stir in the wine and carrots and cook until liquid evaporates, about 15 minutes.

2 Add the chicken broth, white pepper, and nutmeg to the saucepan. Bring to a boil; reduce heat, cover, and simmer until carrots are tender, about 20 minutes.

3 Puree the carrot mixture in a food processor. Add the milk and blend until very smooth. Rinse and dry the saucepan. Return the soup to the pan and cook over low heat until warmed through. Serve immediately, garnishing with minced fresh chives.

SILKY TOMATO GAZPACHO

Most gazpacho recipes are chunky, but this version is silky and elegant, garnished with minced cucumber and a drizzle of fine extra-virgin olive oil. For a colorful variation, use ripe, flavorful yellow tomatoes and yellow bell peppers.

3 pounds ripe red tomatoes, cored, peeled, and coarsely chopped (page 151)

2 large slices of day-old French or Italian bread, crusts removed, cut into 1-inch cubes

2 red bell peppers, peeled, seeded, deribbed, and diced (page 151)

1 cucumber (about ½ pound), peeled, seeded, and finely diced, 4 tablespoons reserved for garnish

1 large clove garlic, minced

½ small red onion, diced

¼ cup extra-virgin olive oil, plus more for drizzling

¼ cup sherry wine vinegar or champagne vinegar

½ teaspoon sweet Hungarian paprika

2½ teaspoons fine sea salt

Freshly ground black pepper for garnish

1 In a large bowl combine all of the ingredients except for the cucumber garnish and toss well to combine. Let stand at room temperature for 1 hour to draw the juices out of the vegetables.

2 Transfer the mixture in batches to a blender or food processor and process until very smooth. Strain in a large, fine-mesh sieve set over another large bowl or a glass 2-quart measuring cup, pressing on the solids with the back of a spoon or ladle. Discard the solids and repeat with the remaining mixture until complete. Add more salt to taste.

3 Cover the bowl with plastic wrap and chill in the refrigerator for at least 2 hours. To serve, ladle the soup into chilled bowls. Garnish with the reserved diced cucumber, a sprinkle of freshly ground pepper, and drizzle each serving with additional extra-virgin olive oil.

This is a refreshing, cool soup to serve on hot summer days. Although it tastes rich and creamy, it is low-calorie and gets its silken texture from fat-free yogurt and nutritious avocados. It's a lovely pale green, one of the prettiest colors on our palette. Fresh chives and chive flowers from the garden make a pretty and flavorful garnish.

2 tablespoons butter

1 cup diced yellow onion

2 cups peeled, seeded, and diced cucumber

2 cups fat-free chicken broth

2 cups plain fat-free yogurt

1 ripe Hass avocado, peeled, pit removed,
    and diced

Fine sea salt

6 tablespoons low-fat sour cream, optional

4 tablespoons minced chives for garnish

3 chive flowers

Let us be grateful to people who make us happy; they are the charming gardeners who make our souls blossom. —MARCEL PROUST

1 In a large saucepan over medium heat, melt the butter and sauté the onions until softened, about 10 minutes. Add the cucumber and chicken broth and simmer for 30 minutes until the cucumber is very soft. Remove pan from heat and let cool for 15 to 30 minutes.

2 Puree the soup in a food processor until very smooth. Add the yogurt and avocado and process until well blended. Add sea salt to taste. Transfer to a large pitcher and cover the top with plastic wrap. Chill in the refrigerator for at least 2 hours or overnight.

3 Pour into chilled cups. Drop a tablespoon of sour cream onto the soup in each cup and garnish with chives and chive florets that have been plucked from the chive flowers.

We plant lots of zucchini in our garden and in early summer are rewarded with the first of many zucchini flowers. We avoid picking the short-stemmed female flowers that bear the zucchini later in the summer, and harvest the longer-stemmed male flowers for painting and cooking. If possible, pick the zucchini blossoms just before serving so they are nice and fresh. Laying the blossoms on top of the grated cheese keeps them afloat in this flavorful vegetable soup. Besides being tasty, the blossoms are fun to paint. When cut in half, we can observe all the parts of the flower and illustrate it as a botanical study.

8 cups chicken broth

4 tablespoons butter

2 tablespoons extra-virgin olive oil

2 medium carrots, diced

2 medium yellow onions, diced

2 celery stalks, thinly sliced

2 medium zucchini, diced

2 cups dried penne pasta

Fine sea salt

Freshly ground black pepper

Grated Parmigiano-Reggiano cheese

8 zucchini blossoms, cut in half lengthwise,
    stamens removed

You cannot grow just one zucchini. Minutes after you plant a single seed, hundreds of zucchini will barge out of the ground and sprawl around the garden. . . . At night, you will be able to hear the ground quake as more and more zucchinis erupt.

—DAVE BARRY

1 Bring the chicken broth to a boil in a medium-size soup pot.

2 Meanwhile, heat the butter and olive oil in a large frying pan and add the carrots, onions, and celery. Cook over medium-low heat, stirring occasionally, for 15 minutes, until the onions become slightly transparent. Add the zucchini and cook for about 3 minutes, and then add the vegetable mixture to the chicken broth in the soup pot.

3 Return the soup to a boil, and then add the pasta and cook for about 11 minutes, until pasta is al dente.

4 Season the soup with salt and pepper to taste. Ladle into eight soup dishes. Top with grated Parmigiano-Reggiano cheese and zucchini blossoms.

At the end of summer corn is ready to be picked. I like to grow the sweet bicolored corn. For this recipe, I prefer fresh corn to frozen. Pick the corn right before cooking and refrigerate it until you're ready to make the soup.

10 medium ears sweet corn, husks and silk removed

4 slices applewood-smoked bacon

1½ cups green onions, both white and green parts, trimmed and chopped into small dice

½ cup celery, cut into ½-inch dice

2 pounds small yellow summer squash, trimmed and cut into ½-inch dice

4½ cups whole milk

2 teaspoons minced fresh thyme leaves

1 teaspoon fine sea salt

½ teaspoon freshly ground black pepper

1 With a sharp knife, slice the kernels from the cobs of corn. Reserve ½ cup of the kernels for garnish, then divide the rest of the kernels into two bowls and set aside.

2 In a large, uncovered soup pot over medium heat, cook the bacon until crispy. Remove the bacon from the pot and transfer to paper towels to drain. When cool, crumble the bacon and set aside.

3 In the same pot, add half of the chopped green onions to the bacon drippings along with the celery and squash. Sauté over medium heat for 10 to 13 minutes until the vegetables are tender.

4 In a blender or food processor, place half of the corn kernels and half of the milk, along with the thyme, salt, and pepper, and process until smooth. Transfer the puréed mixture and the remaining corn kernels and milk to the soup pot. Stir to combine. Heat pot over medium heat until milk is hot and then cook for 5 minutes, stirring constantly, until the corn kernels are tender but still slightly crunchy. Don't let the soup come to a boil. Taste and add more salt or pepper as desired.

5 When ready to serve, ladle the chowder into soup bowls. Top each serving with some of the bacon and reserved green onions and corn kernels.

CHICKEN VEGETABLE SOUP WITH PASTA SHELLS

This is a very tasty soup that I like to serve at the end of summer when I have extra zucchini, tomatoes, and fresh basil still growing in the garden. Here, I've added uncooked chicken while the soup is being prepared, but you can also add leftover roasted or grilled chicken breasts at the very end just before serving. The secret to this flavorful soup is sautéing the vegetables in butter, but you can easily substitute olive oil as well.

3 tablespoons butter

1 medium zucchini, trimmed and cut into
    ½-inch dice

1 medium onion, peeled and cut into ½-inch dice

1 large carrot, peeled and cut into ½-inch dice

1 stalk celery, cut into ½-inch dice

½ cup diced canned tomatoes

1 teaspoon fresh thyme leaves, or ¼ teaspoon
    dried

8 cups chicken broth

1 whole boneless, skinless chicken breast,
    split into 2 halves and cut into
    ¼-inch-wide strips

1 cup small (½-inch) uncooked pasta shells

¼ cup fresh basil, chopped

Fine sea salt

Freshly ground black pepper

Freshly grated Parmigiano-Reggiano cheese,
    for garnish

1. In a large soup pot melt the butter over medium heat. Add the zucchini, onion, carrots, and celery and sauté for 10 minutes, or until softened.

2. Add the tomatoes, thyme, broth, and chicken. Cover and bring to a boil, then reduce heat, remove lid, and simmer for 15 minutes.

3. Stir in the pasta and cook until just tender, about 10 minutes.

4. Stir in the basil, salt, and pepper to taste. Serve immediately with the grated cheese at the table.

MINESTRONE WITH ROSEMARY-GARLIC OIL

Serves 8

I like to serve this soup on a cool autumn or winter day. It is hearty, rich, and delicious. The secret ingredient is a flavored olive oil I add just before serving, made with our Tuscan rosemary and garlic. The heat of the soup releases the perfumed oils of the rosemary and garlic for a last-minute touch of Mediterranean flavor, and the added oil gives the soup a richer taste.

1 large yellow onion, peeled and cut into small dice

1 medium carrot, peeled and cut into small dice

3 medium stalks of celery, trimmed and cut into small dice

1 medium baking potato, peeled and cut into ½-inch cubes

1 medium zucchini, trimmed and diced

6 white mushrooms, washed, trimmed, and sliced

3 cups Swiss chard (ribs discarded), chopped

One 28-ounce can of whole tomatoes, drained and chopped

8 cups chicken broth

One 2- by 4-inch piece of Parmigiano-Reggiano cheese rind

ROSEMARY-GARLIC OIL

1 tablespoon fresh rosemary

1 teaspoon minced garlic

1 tablespoon extra-virgin olive oil

Fine sea salt

Freshly ground black pepper

Freshly grated Parmigiano-Reggiano cheese

1 Bring the vegetables, tomatoes, chicken broth, and cheese rind to a boil in a large soup pot. Reduce the heat to medium-low and simmer, uncovered, stirring occasionally, for about 1 hour until vegetables are tender. Remove and discard the cheese rind.

2 Using a small food processor or a large knife, mince the rosemary. Remove the minced rosemary to a small bowl, and then stir in the garlic and olive oil.

3 Stir the Rosemary-Garlic Oil into the soup. Add salt and pepper to taste. Ladle soup into bowls and serve immediately. Pass the grated cheese for sprinkling over the soup.

Butternut Squash-Apple Soup

Serves 8

I love butternut squash soup. The color and texture of this soup is so rich that every time I make it, I feel like dipping my brush into it to paint with it. The addition of apples and apple cider vinegar gives the soup a wonderful sweet-and-sour flavor that my students always find unique.

8 tablespoons unsalted butter

1 cup maple syrup

3 pounds butternut squash, peeled and cubed

4 Fuji apples, peeled, cored, and cubed

8 cups chicken broth

1 cup apple cider vinegar

1 teaspoon salt

1 teaspoon ground sage

1 teaspoon cinnamon

½ teaspoon ground cloves

¼ teaspoon freshly ground nutmeg

½ cup heavy cream, for garnish

1 In a soup pot over medium heat, melt the butter with the maple syrup. Add the squash and sauté for 15 minutes.

2 Add the apples, broth, vinegar, salt, sage, and spices. Bring to a boil. Reduce heat, cover, and simmer until apples are tender, about 30 minutes.

3 Let cool slightly, then purée in batches in a blender or food processor until smooth. Return the purée to the pot and heat gently, but do not allow to boil.

4 When ready to serve, ladle into soup plates. Garnish each serving with a drizzle of heavy cream.

Of all the varieties of mushrooms available, shiitakes are my favorite. I use white button mushrooms for the base of this soup, but add sautéed shiitakes as a garnish, giving this soup a rich mushroom flavor.

8 tablespoons unsalted butter, divided

6 large shallots, minced

2 cloves garlic, minced

½ teaspoon ground nutmeg

2 pounds white button mushrooms,
    washed, dried, and thinly sliced

7 cups chicken broth

⅓ cup dry sherry

1 cup heavy cream

2 teaspoons lemon juice

Fine sea salt

Freshly ground black pepper

8 ounces shiitake mushrooms, cleaned,
    stems removed, and thinly sliced

1 Melt 6 tablespoons butter in a large soup pot over medium-low heat. Add shallots and sauté, stirring frequently, for 4 minutes. Stir in garlic and nutmeg and cook for 1 minute. Increase heat to medium, add sliced button mushrooms, and cook, stirring occasionally, for 20 minutes. Pour the chicken broth into the mushroom mixture and simmer for another 15 to 20 minutes.

2 Puree the soup in batches in a blender until smooth. Return the soup to the pot and bring to a simmer over low heat. Stir in the sherry, cream, and lemon juice. Season to taste with salt and pepper.

3 Meanwhile, heat remaining 2 tablespoons butter in a medium skillet over low heat. When foam subsides, add the shiitake mushrooms and sprinkle with salt and pepper to taste. Cover and cook, stirring occasionally, for about 10 minutes. Uncover and continue to cook, until the liquid from the mushrooms has evaporated and the mushrooms have browned.

4 Serve soup in bowls, garnishing each serving with the sautéed shiitake mushrooms.

THE WINTER GARDEN

In winter, our mountain is colder and wetter than the coast nearby. It's the season in which I think and plan for next year's garden. I search through seed catalogs, keep my worm bin happy, turn the soil, and replenish compost in the beds. It's time to clean and cut back old growth. With the cold winter rains, some things grow—peas, kale, and fava beans. I grow a few baby lettuces inside warm garden cloches, and this year I planted more asparagus to winter over, to increase the size of the bed. I'll plant potatoes and my favorite bok choy, just because they taste better than store-bought. And I'll save dried seedpods and leaves off the vines for painting. Because I don't spend as much time in the garden, I have more personal time to paint. I teach classes in painted journals and share my collection of birds' nests with students to paint from. I make hot, comforting soups for my classes and we paint, staying warm in our cozy studio nest, waiting for spring to come.

Salads

Mixed Greens and Strawberry Salad with Almonds
    and Creamy Orange Dressing   46

Fennel, Blood Orange, and Grilled Chicken
    Salad with Candied Walnuts   51

"Dutch Masters" Chicken Salad with
    Red Grapes and Toasted Pecans   52

Quinoa Salad with Grilled Chicken, Dried
    Pineapple, and Toasted Pistachios   55

Rice Noodle Salad "Nests" with
    Julienned Vegetables and Prawns   56

Flower Petal Salad   61

Pan-Seared Sea Scallop Salad in Giant Scallop
    Shells with Citrus-Herb Vinaigrette   64

Caesar Salad with Lemon-Grilled Chicken   69

Mediterranean Salmon Pasta Salad   73

Prawn, Mango, Melon, and Cucumber Salad
    with Lemon Vinaigrette   74

Garden Bento Boxes: Quail Eggs on
    Frisée "Nests"   79

Mixed Green Salad with Pears,
    Macadamia Nuts, and Brie   81

Fresh Fig and Crispy Prosciutto Salad   82

Smoked Turkey and Romaine Salad with
    Avocado-Lime Dressing   85

Autumn Salad with Persimmons and Feta Cheese   87

MIXED GREENS AND STRAWBERRY SALAD WITH ALMONDS AND CREAMY ORANGE DRESSING

Serves 4

This colorful spring salad is inspired by the arrival of the first red strawberries to ripen in late February and early March. When I serve the salad to my painting classes, we pick enough berries from the garden to paint and to eat. The plants continue to bear fruit throughout the spring, as do the acres of field strawberries from local farms up and down our Northern California coast.

DRESSING

½ cup mayonnaise

½ cup frozen orange juice concentrate, thawed

1 tablespoon orange marmalade

1 small head butter lettuce, leaves separated and washed, dried, and chilled

3 to 4 ounces mixed baby lettuces, washed, dried, and chilled

2 cups strawberries, washed, hulled, and sliced

¼ cup sliced almonds, toasted (page 151)

Fine sea salt

Freshly ground black pepper

1 To make the dressing: In a medium bowl, whisk together the mayonnaise and orange juice concentrate until combined. Add the marmalade and whisk again until well blended. Store covered in the refrigerator until ready to use.

2 Reserve 4 large whole leaves of butter lettuce for plating. Carefully tear the remaining leaves into bite-size pieces.

3 To assemble the salads, spoon 1 tablespoon of dressing in the center of each of 4 serving plates (tip: this enables the salad to have enough dressing while keeping it fresh-looking right up until serving). Place a whole, large leaf of butter lettuce off-center on the plate. Scatter a handful of torn butter lettuce and a handful of mixed baby greens over the entire plate. Scatter ½ cup sliced strawberries and 1 tablespoon of sliced almonds over the greens. Drizzle each salad with an additional tablespoon of dressing and sprinkle with salt and pepper to taste. Serve immediately, with remaining dressing in a bowl or small pitcher on the table to add if desired.

ABOVE AND RIGHT: Because we enjoy so many colorful salads at our meals and classes, we devote a large section of the garden to lettuces, especially delicate butter lettuce, which pairs well with fresh berries and citrus fruit. Strawberries are one of the easiest fruits to paint, but it's hard not to eat them when they're sitting beside your brushes and palette. Our area of Northern California is famous for producing large, juicy, flavorful berries. One local producer, Swanton Berry Farm in Pescadero, also invites customers to pick their own. In our garden, we grow the same plump berries in large wine barrel planters to protect them from garden pests and save room for the tiny alpine strawberries as well.

One must ask children and birds how cherries and strawberries taste. —Johann Wolfgang Von Goethe

Fennel, Blood Orange, and Grilled Chicken Salad with Candied Walnuts

In California, blood oranges are available from November until May. They are so vibrant to paint and delicious in salads. This salad is a favorite with my students. The Orange Champagne Vinaigrette used on the salad is delicious; I like to make a good quantity of it to have on hand for other salads. To make a creamy version of this dressing, I add mayonnaise.

Orange Champagne Vinaigrette

¼ cup extra-virgin olive oil

¼ cup Orange Champagne Vinegar (page 150)

Fine sea salt

Freshly ground black pepper

2 whole boneless, skinless chicken breasts,
    split into 4 halves

1 tablespoon extra-virgin olive oil

1 clove garlic, crushed

Fine sea salt

Freshly ground black pepper

1 small head Bibb or butter lettuce

1 fennel bulb, halved and sliced thin, fronds reserved

4 blood oranges, peeled and segmented (page 151)

½ cup Candied Walnuts (page 152)

2 ounces Parmigiano-Reggiano cheese, thinly sliced
    with a vegetable peeler

1 Prepare the dressing: Pour olive oil, Orange Champagne Vinegar, and salt and pepper to taste into a lidded jar and shake until emulsified. Refrigerate until ready to use, up to 1 week.

2 In a large, shallow dish, rub chicken breasts with olive oil and crushed garlic, and sprinkle with salt and pepper to taste.

3 In a stovetop grill pan over medium-high heat, grill the chicken for 8 to 10 minutes on each side or until no longer pink inside. Remove chicken from the pan and cool. Slice into narrow strips.

4 Divide lettuce between four plates. Evenly distribute the sliced fennel, orange segments, chicken, and Candied Walnuts among the four salads. Spoon Orange Champagne Vinaigrette over each salad. Top with cheese shavings and fennel fronds.

"Dutch Masters" Chicken Salad with Red Grapes and Toasted Pecans

Serves 4

One of my students' favorite classes is learning to paint fruit and flowers in the style of the Dutch Masters with gouache. This beautiful salad with jewel-colored grapes, colorful greens, and toasted pecans was inspired by the ingredients and colors in Dutch still lifes from the eighteenth century, like those of Jan Van Huysum. Naturally, I serve it at these classes in honor of the Old Masters!

2 whole boneless, skinless chicken breasts, split
  into 4 halves (about 1½ pounds)

Fine sea salt

Freshly ground black pepper

1 tablespoon extra-virgin olive oil

½ cup diced celery

1 cup halved seedless red grapes

½ cup pecan halves, toasted (page 151)

12-ounce jar blue cheese dressing (such as
  Toby's brand)

3 cups mixed salad greens

1 cup radicchio leaves, torn into bite-size pieces

1 Season the chicken with salt and pepper. Heat a large pan over medium-high heat. Add the olive oil and then place the chicken breasts into the hot pan. Cook until they are golden, about 5 to 6 minutes per side. Set aside to cool.

2 Cut the chicken into ½-inch cubes. In a large bowl, combine the chicken, celery, grapes, and pecans. Toss with the blue cheese dressing, cover with plastic wrap, and refrigerate until cold, about an hour. When ready to serve, divide the salad greens and radicchio equally among four serving plates. Top each serving with an equal amount of chicken salad and serve immediately.

Quinoa Salad with Grilled Chicken, Dried Pineapple, and Toasted Pistachios

Serves 4

This tasty main course salad has an Asian flair, seasoned with ginger, cumin, and sesame oil. I like to serve it as a complement to my art classes on painting Asian vegetables like bok choy, snow peas, ginger root, and cilantro, many of which we grow in the garden.

1¼ cups uncooked organic quinoa, rinsed thoroughly with cold water

2 cups chicken broth

½ cup pistachios, toasted (page 151)

1¼ cups diced grilled, skinless, boneless chicken breast (about ½ pound)

1 to 2 tablespoons chopped chives, to taste

½ cup chopped dried pineapple

1½ tablespoons toasted sesame oil

½ teaspoon ground ginger

¾ teaspoon ground cumin

½ teaspoon fine sea salt

4 cups mixed salad greens

1 In a large saucepan over medium-high heat, bring the quinoa and chicken broth to a boil. Reduce the heat, cover, and simmer for 15 minutes, until all the liquid is absorbed. Remove from the heat and let cool to room temperature.

2 When cooled, fluff the quinoa with a large fork. Add pistachios, diced chicken, chives, dried pineapple, sesame oil, ginger, cumin, and salt and toss well to combine. (Quinoa mixture can be made and stored in the refrigerator up to 8 hours ahead. Bring to room temperature before serving.)

3 To serve, place one cup of salad greens on each of 4 serving plates, making a small well in the center of the greens. Place a mound of the quinoa mixture into each well, dividing equally among the plates. Serve immediately.

Rice Noodle Salad "Nests" with Julienned Vegetables and Prawns

I like to serve this salad during our nest-painting classes. Playing on the theme of birds' nests, butter lettuce leaves hold this flavorful noodle salad topped with vegetables and prawns in a spicy Thai dressing. The nest-like appearance of this main course salad always delights my students.

Dressing

½ cup fish sauce

½ cup freshly squeezed lime juice, from about
    3 to 4 large limes

4 teaspoons light brown sugar

¼ cup red Thai curry paste

1 pound large prawns (approximately 24 to
    28 per pound), poached, cleaned, and chilled
    (page 152)

1 English cucumber, peeled, seeded, and julienned

2 carrots, julienned

1 celery stalk, julienned

A large handful of fresh cilantro, finely chopped

12 ounces dried rice vermicelli noodles

2 heads butter lettuce, leaves separated and
    washed, dried, and chilled

6 sprigs mint

1 In a medium bowl, combine all the dressing ingredients and whisk until the sugar dissolves. Add the prawns, cucumber, carrot, celery, and cilantro and toss well to combine. Cover bowl with plastic wrap and refrigerate until ready to serve.

2 In a large heatproof bowl, cover vermicelli with boiling water. Let soak for 2 to 3 minutes until the noodles are tender. Drain noodles, rinse them with cool water, and drain again.

3 To assemble the salad "nests," place a few lettuce leaves in a circle on each serving plate. Arrange a circle of noodles in the center of the lettuce leaves to resemble a nest. Spoon some of the prawn and vegetable mixture in the middle of the noodles, arranging the prawns on top of the vegetables, and garnish with a sprig of mint. Serve immediately.

A Painter's Flowering Herb Garden Plan

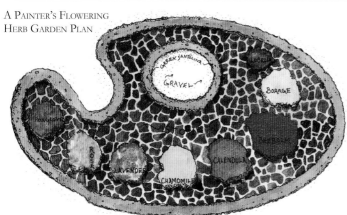

I perhaps owe having become a painter to flowers.

—Claude Monet

Left and above: Like an artist's palette, flowers provide color and visual interest in the garden. Many are also edible and can be used to add color and subtle flavor to foods. Some of the flowers we love to grow and eat are *(clockwise from far left)* blue cornflowers, nasturtiums, roses, scented geraniums, purple chives, and bright orange calendula. They attract not only painters and cooks, but also beneficial bees and butterflies that pollinate the other plants and flowering trees in the garden.

Flower Petal Salad

I grow many different flowers in my garden—some to ward off garden pests, some for recipe garnishes, and some as subjects for painting. My flower-painting workshop is one of the most popular classes of the year. When my students arrive in the morning, we go out to the garden with baskets and cut the flowers we want to paint that day. I provide the group with an array of vessels to choose from, and each student composes a flower arrangement to set beside his or her paints and canvases. The colorful selection of flowers also provides petals for my Flower Petal Salad, which I serve for lunch during the class.

When using in a recipe, make sure flowers are edible and organic, have not been sprayed with insecticides, and have been gently washed and dried. This flower petal salad is so colorful that I like to present it in a large glass salad bowl so that all the flowers can show off their colors. The dressing makes more than needed for this salad, so save the extra for another day.

CREAMY MEYER LEMON DRESSING
1 cup plain yogurt
½ cup mayonnaise
Zest and juice of 1 Meyer lemon
4 tablespoons extra-virgin olive oil
Fine sea salt

6 handfuls (10 to 12 ounces) small-leafed lettuce (such as the inner leaves of green and red butter lettuce)
½ cup unsprayed edible flower petals (such as calendulas, nasturtiums, roses, borage, and violets), plus more for garnish if desired
1 bunch radishes, or a mixture of small red radishes and one larger watermelon radish

1 In a small bowl, combine all the dressing ingredients. Store, covered, in refrigerator for up to three days.

2 Place lettuce into a large glass salad bowl. Sprinkle flower petals on top, then carefully mix them into the salad. Thinly slice the radishes and add them to the salad bowl. To keep the salad looking its best, serve the dressing on the side in a small bowl, and just before serving carefully mix the dressing into the salad. Sprinkle more flower petals on top if desired.

THE SPRING GARDEN

Our garden reawakens in spring. The weather is softer, gentler. My flowers begin to bloom, the butterflies are out and about, bees are buzzing, and birds are singing. My sweet peas have wintered over with strong vines reaching to the top of their netted trellis, tendrils stretching to hold on and climb even further. I can't wait for the first blossoms to appear; their fragrance is intoxicating as the flowers open. I begin planting lettuce in neat rows, and get early tomatoes started along with zucchini and beans. My peas have been in the ground since winter—the sweet petit pois—tiny little peas that jump out of their pods. The first strawberries are basking in the sun and the asparagus spears begin to shoot out of the ground. All my flowers are usually in so that we have enough to paint from and add to our spring salads, lasting through the summer. It's time to think about special recipes to serve to my students for lunch. Strawberries in salads and desserts, and asparagus frittatas are our favorites.

Pan-Seared Sea Scallop Salad in Giant Scallop Shells
with Citrus-Herb Vinaigrette

When we paint shells I like to serve a seafood-themed salad. Serving sea scallops in large scallop shells makes a lovely presentation. Using fresh herbs from our herb garden adds fragrance and texture to the dressing, along with the zest of Meyer lemons. If you don't have large scallop shells (available at cooking shops), just mound the scallops on top of the salad greens on a pretty salad plate.

¼ cup plus ½ cup extra-virgin olive oil

1½ pounds sea scallops

Fine sea salt

Freshly ground black pepper

3 tablespoons Meyer lemon juice, plus lemon zest
    for garnish

2 tablespoons mixed chopped fresh herbs (such
    as parsley, chives, oregano, and thyme)

1 teaspoon Dijon mustard

½ to 1 teaspoon honey, to taste

1 head frisée lettuce, tender inner leaves only

6 ounces mixed baby greens

1. In a large skillet, heat the ¼ cup olive oil over medium heat. Lightly season the scallops with salt and pepper. When the oil is hot, place the scallops in the pan and cook, tossing gently, for 5 minutes, until scallops are opaque. Remove them to a plate and set aside to cool.

2. In a small bowl, combine the remaining ½ cup olive oil, the lemon juice, herbs, mustard, and honey, and whisk until a thick emulsion forms. Adjust ingredients to taste, if necessary.

3. Place scallops in a medium bowl, add the dressing, and toss to coat. Store covered with plastic wrap until ready to serve.

4. Place a little frisée and a handful of mixed baby greens into each of 6 large scallop shells or salad plates. Spoon the dressed scallops on top of the greens. Drizzle some dressing over the salad, sprinkle lemon zest on top, and serve.

PAINTING SEASHELLS

I like to teach painting seashells in the summertime when we all have warm, sandy beaches and lazy beachcombing on our minds. Because I live so close to the ocean, I have long been inspired by the gifts of the sea—shells, sea creatures, seaweed, and sand. Over the years I've amassed a large collection of seashells and different types of sand that I keep in my studio to share with students.

The beautiful shapes, colors, and textures of seashells rank them among nature's finest creations. One of the pleasures of painting shells is that the artist is forced to more carefully observe their infinite variety and complexity. With spots or stripes, and opalescent or chalky surfaces, seashells challenge an artist to record a miniature universe of pattern and texture. I liken them to underwater flowers that have washed ashore.

Shells have been the source of creative inspiration in art for centuries. Think of Botticelli's Venus standing on her giant clamshell rising out of the sea. Leonardo da Vinci's design for a double-spiral staircase is thought to have been inspired by the spiraling forms of a univalve shell. And architectural motifs of scallop shells have adorned the lintels of European doorways and windows and formed the vessels of decorative fountains for centuries.

In the garden, I like to use seashells to line garden paths. I use crushed oyster shells as a soil amendment to add calcium and to neutralize soil acidity. And a giant clamshell makes an excellent birdbath. In the kitchen, I'm inspired to serve salads and hors d'oeuvres in big scallop shells, decorate cookies with sand dollar designs and sand-like sugar, and use shell-shaped noodles in soups and pasta dishes. When I have a shell-painting class, I often include something inspired by seashells on the class lunch menu, which always delights my students. Seashells reconnect us to the natural world and inspire creativity in our work.

CAESAR SALAD WITH LEMON-GRILLED CHICKEN

When my parents were on their honeymoon in Mexico in 1932, they discovered a restaurant that served the most delicious salad. My mom, who was a very good cook, asked the chef-restaurateur, Caesar Cardini, for the recipe, which he graciously gave. For years to come, my mom made this salad for us when we were growing up, and I have continued making it for my own family and students using this recipe. Caesar Salad, named after its creator, has become very popular and can be found in hundreds of cookbooks and restaurants with many variations. The only modification I have made since first making it is the substitution of mayonnaise for raw eggs in the dressing. I also add grilled chicken or pepper-crusted smoked salmon to make it a main-course salad.

1 large head romaine lettuce, leaves separated

GARLIC CROUTONS

3 tablespoons butter

3 tablespoons extra-virgin olive oil

3 cups sourdough French bread, crusts removed, cut into ½-inch cubes

2 large cloves garlic, minced

LEMON-GRILLED CHICKEN

6 tablespoons olive oil

4 large cloves garlic, crushed in a garlic press

2 teaspoons minced fresh thyme leaves

1¼ teaspoons fine sea salt

½ teaspoon freshly ground black pepper

Zest of 1 lemon

2 whole boneless, skinless chicken breasts, split into 4 halves (about 1¾ pounds)

DRESSING

2 tablespoons mayonnaise

3 tablespoons fresh lemon juice

Zest of one lemon

1 tablespoon Dijon mustard

1 tablespoon Worcestershire sauce

½ cup extra-virgin olive oil

1 clove garlic, crushed

4 anchovy fillets, drained and finely chopped

½ cup freshly grated Parmigiano-Reggiano cheese

1 Wash the lettuce and spin in a salad spinner or pat dry with a towel. Roll loosely in a dry dishtowel and place into a large plastic bag and refrigerate for several hours to crisp.

2 To make the croutons, heat the butter and oil in a large skillet over medium-high heat. Add the bread cubes and cook, tossing constantly,

(continued)

for 10 minutes or until golden brown. Remove the pan from the burner. Add the garlic, tossing constantly, for 1 to 2 minutes. Remove croutons from the pan and let cool.

3 To make the chicken, combine all the ingredients except the chicken in a 1-gallon zipper-top bag or a large bowl. Add the chicken breasts and massage the marinade into the chicken with your hands. Seal the bag or, if using a bowl, cover bowl with plastic wrap. Marinate the chicken in the refrigerator for at least 4 hours or up to 12 hours. Remove from refrigerator 30 minutes before grilling.

4 Place a grill pan over high heat. Remove the chicken breasts from the marinade and grill 5 minutes per side or until cooked through. Transfer the chicken from the pan to a cutting board and let cool. Cut each breast crosswise into ¼-inch-thick slices and set them aside.

5 To make the dressing, in a medium bowl whisk together the mayonnaise, lemon juice and zest, mustard, and Worcestershire sauce until blended. Slowly drizzle in the olive oil while whisking. Stir in the garlic and anchovies and set aside.

6 To serve, tear the chilled lettuce leaves into bite-size pieces and place them into a large salad bowl. Add the dressing and toss well. Add the chicken slices and Parmesan cheese and gently toss again. Top with croutons and serve immediately, dividing among four individual serving plates.

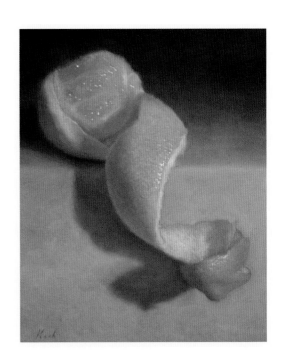

I once gave a class on painting the watery cityscapes of Venice in the style of the artist John Singer Sargent. We studied his watercolor techniques from his study entitled "On The Grand Canal." To add to the Venetian experience, I served this seafood pasta salad seasoned with olive oil and Meyer lemons from the tree in our garden. I like to use peppered smoked salmon, but any smoked salmon will work.

¾ pound orecchiette pasta

7 ounces smoked salmon, torn into bite-size pieces

½ teaspoon dried oregano

3 green onions, thinly sliced

12 pitted Kalamata olives, sliced in half

Juice and zest from 1 to 2 Meyer lemons (about
    3 to 4 tablespoons juice)

½ cup sundried tomatoes, chopped

1 tablespoon capers, rinsed and drained

6 tablespoons extra-virgin olive oil

1 tablespoon minced garlic

Fine sea salt

Freshly ground black pepper

¾ cup crumbled feta cheese

1 Bring a large pot of salted water to a boil. Add the pasta and cook until *al dente*, about 10 minutes. Drain and set aside to cool.

2 In a large bowl, toss the pasta with the smoked salmon, oregano, green onions, olives, lemon juice and zest, sundried tomatoes, capers, olive oil, garlic, and salt and pepper to taste. Divide among four individual plates and serve with the crumbled feta in a bowl to add at the table.

All gardening is landscape painting. —HORACE WALPOLE

PRAWN, MANGO, MELON, AND CUCUMBER SALAD WITH LEMON VINAIGRETTE

Serves 6

Several years ago I hosted one of my painting workshops in Italy. This salad is inspired by a memorable salad I had while staying at a villa on Lake Como, north of Milan. It is fresh, light, and lemony—a perfect light lunch for a hot summer day!

1 mango

1 cantaloupe

1 English cucumber

3 Roma tomatoes

6 ounces baby arugula leaves

1 small head frisée lettuce, inner leaves only, torn into bite-size pieces

1 pound medium prawns (about 18 to 24 per pound), poached, cleaned, and chilled (page 152)

DRESSING

½ cup extra-virgin olive oil

Juice and zest of 1 lemon

1 clove garlic, crushed

Fine sea salt

Fresh ground black pepper

1 With a large knife, cutting lengthwise, close to the pit of the mango, cut a large slice from one side of the fruit. Cut another large slice from the opposite side. Without breaking the skin, score the inside flesh into small cubes with the tip of the knife. Push the skin inside out with your fingers to expose the cubes, and cut them away from the skin. Place the mango cubes in a large bowl.

2 Cut the cantaloupe in half and remove the seeds with a spoon. Slice the melon halves into eight wedges, and then cut off the rinds. Cut the wedges into small cubes and add them to the large bowl.

3 Peel and quarter the cucumber lengthwise, removing the seeds. Cut the wedges into small cubes and add to the large bowl.

4 Thinly slice each tomato into julienne strips and add to the bowl. Chill the mixture, covered with plastic wrap, until ready to serve.

(continued)

PRAWN, MANGO, MELON, AND CUCUMBER SALAD
WITH LEMON VINAIGRETTE (CONTINUED)

5 When ready to serve, wash the arugula and frisée. Pat dry with paper towels or dry in a salad spinner. Divide the arugula and frisée evenly among the serving plates. Top each serving with a generous portion of the fruit mixture and add 3 or 4 chilled prawns.

6 In a small bowl, whisk together the dressing ingredients and drizzle evenly over the salads. Serve immediately.

'Just living is not enough,' said the butterfly.
'One must have sunshine, freedom, and a little flower.'
—HANS CHRISTIAN ANDERSEN

Garden Bento Boxes: Quail Eggs on Frisée "Nests"

One of my most popular classes in recent years has been painting little boxes of natural curiosities. Dating from the Renaissance, cabinets of curiosities were a method of displaying a variety of natural objects—which might include eggs, nests, bones, geological specimens, shells, insects, and dried plants—in a compartmented box or cabinet to show off a collection of natural wonders. I created these box lunches to celebrate our painting theme. For the serving container, you will need a plastic or wooden bento box, available in Asian markets, or a food container with 2- to 3-inch sides.

12 quail eggs

1 pound frisée lettuce

½ cup purchased seafood cocktail sauce

1 pound medium prawns (about 18 to 24 per pound), poached, cleaned, and chilled (page 152)

12 cherry tomatoes

1 bunch scallions, trimmed

1 bunch baby radishes

4 ounces mâche or tatsoi leaves

1 roasted red bell pepper, cut in wide strips (page 151)

⅛ cup capers, drained

¼ cup black olives

½ cup Champagne Orange Vinaigrette (page 51)

Bread sticks (optional)

1 Fill a medium pot with cold water and gently place the quail eggs at the bottom. Over medium-high heat, bring the water to a boil and cook the eggs for 2 minutes. Remove the pot from the heat and carefully transfer the eggs to a bowl to cool.

2 To assemble the bento boxes, arrange the frisée into the shape of a nest in the largest compartment of the serving boxes. (If using a container without compartments, use little teacups to create compartments within the container.) Spoon 2 tablespoons of cocktail sauce in a tiny bowl or teacup and top with 4 prawns. Place the prawn bowl and individual portions of the tomatoes, scallions, and radishes in the other compartments.

3 Make mâche or tatsoi bouquets by arranging the leaves in little clusters and placing a curled strip of red pepper and the capers and olives in the centers. Nestle the bouquets in the spaces between the other items. Drizzle the vegetables and frisée with 2 tablespoons of the vinaigrette, then place 3 quail eggs in the middle of each "nest," and tuck a few breadsticks in the side of the box if desired.

Mixed Green Salad with Pears, Macadamia Nuts, and Brie

Serves 4

Pears are one of the loveliest fruits to paint, coming in many different shades of green, yellow, gold, and crimson, and sometimes tinged with pink or red. They are also the stars of this simple fall salad served with toasted macadamia nuts and wedges of Brie. Use any type of ripe pear in season.

1 cup unsalted macadamia nuts

4 firm-ripe pears

Juice of 1 lime

4 large handfuls mixed salad greens

¼ cup extra-virgin olive oil

Fine sea salt

8 ounces Brie cheese, cut into 8 wedges

1 baguette, sliced

One is wise to cultivate the tree that bears fruit in our soul. —Henry David Thoreau

1 Preheat oven to 400°F. Place the nuts on a rimmed baking sheet or in a small, shallow baking pan. Toast, stirring occasionally, until very lightly browned and fragrant, approximately 5 to 8 minutes. Watch closely so nuts do not overcook. Remove the nuts from the oven and allow to cool completely. Coarsely chop or halve the nuts.

2 Slice the pears into thin wedges, and then cut away the core. In a large bowl, gently toss the pear slices with the lime juice. Add the mixed greens to the pears and toss again. Divide the greens and pears among four plates. Drizzle each salad with one tablespoon of olive oil, and sprinkle with salt to taste. Top with the toasted nuts. Place 2 wedges of Brie on the side of each plate. Serve with baguette slices.

FRESH FIG AND CRISPY PROSCIUTTO SALAD

When our large brown Turkey figs ripen in the early fall, I like to make this salad to complement the class I teach on painting figs. Any variety of fresh fig will be delicious, but adjust the number of figs you use depending on the size available. Prosciutto always tastes good with figs and, for this salad, I like to crisp it in the oven. Ricotta salata cheese is mild, slightly salty, and easy to crumble or grate. If you can't find it, you can substitute goat cheese or feta.

DRESSING

3 tablespoons fresh lemon juice

1 tablespoon honey

⅛ teaspoon fine sea salt

¼ teaspoon freshly ground black pepper

3 tablespoons extra-virgin olive oil

SALAD

6 ounces very thinly sliced prosciutto

2 large heads butter lettuce, one green and
   one red, leaves separated and washed, dried,
   and chilled

6 to 12 brown Turkey figs or Black Mission figs,
   sliced in half lengthwise

3 to 4 ounces ricotta salata cheese, crumbled

3 tablespoons dry-roasted sunflower seeds

1 In a small bowl, combine the lemon juice, honey, salt, and pepper and whisk well. Gradually drizzle in olive oil, whisking constantly until blended. Set aside.

2 Preheat an oven to 350°F. Arrange the prosciutto slices on a baking pan and bake until just crisp, about 5 to 10 minutes. Remove from the oven and, when cool, crumble into pieces and set aside.

3 When ready to serve, tear the butter lettuce into bite-size pieces and place in a large bowl. Drizzle the dressing over the lettuce and toss gently to coat. Arrange the lettuce on a large serving platter. Scatter the figs, prosciutto, cheese, and sunflower seeds on top and serve immediately.

Smoked Turkey and Romaine Salad
with Avocado-Lime Dressing

This is one of my students' favorite salads. It's the avocado-lime dressing that makes it taste so good. You can also use this dressing as a dip with tortilla chips or sticks of raw carrot and jicama.

Dressing

¼ cup low-fat buttermilk

1 tablespoon mayonnaise

Zest from 1 lime, plus 1 tablespoon fresh
    lime juice

¼ teaspoon fine sea salt

⅛ teaspoon cayenne pepper

1 clove garlic, peeled and coarsely chopped

½ ripe avocado, peeled, seeded, and coarsely
    chopped

4 cups romaine lettuce (from about 1 large head),
    torn into bite-size pieces

2 cups (about 8 ounces) diced smoked turkey

½ cup green onions, thinly sliced

2 tablespoons chopped fresh cilantro

1 To make the dressing, combine all the dressing ingredients in a blender and process until smooth. Set aside, or cover and chill until ready to use, up to four hours ahead.

2 In a large bowl, toss the lettuce with the turkey, green onions, and cilantro. Drizzle the dressing over the salad and gently toss to coat. Divide among four individual plates.

Autumn Salad with Persimmons and Feta Cheese   **Serves 4**

Bright orange persimmons and tangy red cranberries add the colors and fruit of fall to this autumn salad. When using mixed greens for a salad, I like to crisp them by chilling them overnight. To do this, gently wash and dry them the night before serving, then wrap in a towel and store in a large plastic bag in the refrigerator until ready to serve.

¼ cup extra-virgin olive oil

Juice of 1 lemon

4 cups mixed salad greens

4 ripe Fuyu persimmons, peeled, quartered,
    and thinly sliced

4 ounces Feta cheese, crumbled

⅛ cup pine nuts, toasted (page 151)

¼ cup dried cranberries

Fine sea salt

Freshly ground black pepper

1 In a wide bowl, whisk the olive oil and lemon juice together. Add the salad greens and mix to coat with dressing. Mound equal portions on four salad plates.

2 Arrange persimmon slices over the greens on each plate. Sprinkle the crumbled Feta cheese, pine nuts, and cranberries over the salads. Add salt and pepper to taste.

And the fruits will outdo what the flowers have promised. —François de Malherbe

SANDWICHES, PIZZAS & SAVORY TARTS

OPEN-FACED WATERCRESS, NASTURTIUM,
AND CUCUMBER-CREAM CHEESE SANDWICHES 90

CRISPY BACON, ARUGULA, TOMATO, AND
CREAM CHEESE SANDWICHES 93

GRILLED CHICKEN SANDWICHES WITH
SMOKED ALMONDS AND DRIED APRICOTS 94

MOZZARELLA, TOMATO, AND TAPENADE SANDWICHES 95

FRESH FIG AND BLACK FOREST HAM SANDWICHES 96

TOASTED SOURDOUGH CROSTINI TOPPED WITH
WHITE BEAN PURÉE AND SAUTÉED GREENS 99

SMOKED SALMON SANDWICHES WITH
RADISH, CUCUMBER, AND GINGER RELISH 100

CURRIED CHICKEN PITA SANDWICHES WITH
CARROTS AND GOLDEN RAISINS 102

TAHINI-MARINATED CHICKEN SANDWICHES 103

HOME-CURED SALMON WITH HORSERADISH-DILL
CREAM SAUCE 104

MINI PIZZAS WITH ITALIAN PLUM TOMATOES,
RED ONIONS, AND BASIL 109

FOUR-CHEESE PIZZAS WITH MIXED HERBS AND
HERB FLOWERS 110

SPRING ASPARAGUS FRITTATA WITH PEAS AND PEPPERS 113

SUMMER TOMATO TARTS WITH GOAT CHEESE AND MINT 114

BOTANICAL MUSHROOM TART 119

Open-Faced Watercress, Nasturtium, and Cucumber-Cream Cheese Sandwiches

Serves 6

These colorful open-faced sandwiches combine the mildly spicy flavors of watercress and nasturtiums with cream cheese. The variegated colors of nasturtiums are fun to paint so I make sure to plant Dwarf Jewel Mix in my garden. The colors are bright and sunny: yellow, pink, red, and orange—the perfect colors and size for sandwiches and salads.

40 unsprayed nasturtium flowers, washed and dried

1 large bunch of fresh watercress, washed, dried, and large stems removed

8 ounces cream cheese, softened

1 medium cucumber, peeled, seeded, and diced

½ teaspoon fine sea salt

⅛ teaspoon freshly ground black pepper

1 small red onion, thinly sliced

6 slices of hearty whole-grain bread, such as rye, whole wheat, or multi-grain

Bread feeds the body, indeed, but flowers feed also the soul. —The Koran

1 Setting aside 12 nasturtium flowers for garnish, finely julienne the rest with a sharp knife. Setting aside 6 watercress sprigs for garnish, finely chop the remaining watercress.

2 In a medium bowl, mix the cream cheese with the chopped flowers, chopped watercress, cucumber, salt, and pepper. Cover with plastic wrap and chill in the refrigerator for 1 hour to allow the flavors to blend together.

3 Remove the cream cheese mixture from the refrigerator half an hour before serving to allow it to soften slightly. With a sharp knife, finely julienne 6 of the reserved nasturtium flowers. Spread the cream cheese mixture on the bread slices. Top each slice with some red onion slices and a sprinkling of the julienned flowers.

4 To serve, place 1 slice of the prepared bread on each plate, and top with a whole nasturtium flower and a watercress sprig.

CRISPY BACON, ARUGULA, TOMATO, AND CREAM CHEESE SANDWICHES

Serves 6

Peppery arugula is a wonderful alternative to lettuce when making bacon and tomato sandwiches. I grow it year round in the garden. When serving this sandwich for painting classes, I cook the bacon the night before and reheat it in the oven just before assembling the finished sandwiches.

18 slices of applewood smoked bacon

6 sourdough sandwich rolls, halved lengthwise

8 ounces cream cheese

3 large ripe red tomatoes, thinly sliced

3 cups baby arugula

1 In a large frying pan over medium heat, cook the bacon until crispy. Transfer to paper towels to drain.

2 To assemble the sandwiches, spread cream cheese on the cut sides of all the rolls. Top each of the bottom halves of the rolls with a layer of sliced tomatoes, 3 slices of bacon, and ½ cup of arugula. Place the tops of the rolls on each sandwich and slice the sandwiches in half. Serve on a platter or on individual plates.

Cooking is an art, but you eat it too.

—MARCELLA HAZAN

GRILLED CHICKEN SANDWICHES WITH SMOKED ALMONDS AND DRIED APRICOTS

Serves 4

The combination of smoked almonds and dried apricots gives this sandwich a sweet, smoky flavor and a pleasing crunch. If I'm pressed for time, I'll buy grilled chicken from the deli.

½ cup sour cream

2 tablespoons mayonnaise

2 whole boneless, skinless chicken breasts,
    split into 4 halves

1 tablespoon extra-virgin olive oil

¼ teaspoon fine sea salt

⅛ teaspoon freshly ground black pepper

1 cup dried apricots, diced (from a 6-ounce
    package)

⅔ cup chopped celery

¼ cup chopped smoked almonds (such
    as Blue Diamond brand Smokehouse
    Almonds)

1 tablespoon finely chopped green onions

4 French-style sandwich rolls, sliced in half
    horizontally

4 large butter lettuce leaves

1 Combine the sour cream and mayonnaise in a large bowl, stirring until well blended. Set aside.

2 Place a grill pan over medium-high heat. Rinse the chicken breasts in cold water and pat dry with paper towels. Rub the flesh with olive oil, and then sprinkle with the salt and pepper. Grill 5 minutes per side, or until done. Remove to a cutting board. Let chicken cool, then dice it into ¼-inch cubes.

3 Add the chicken to the bowl with the mayonnaise-sour cream mixture. Add the dried apricots, celery, smoked almonds, and green onions. Stir well. Cover with plastic wrap and chill until ready to serve.

4 To serve, spread a quarter of the chicken mixture onto the bottom half of each roll. Top with a lettuce leaf and the other half of the roll. Cut the sandwiches in half and serve.

MOZZARELLA, TOMATO, AND TAPENADE SANDWICHES Serves 4

This sandwich stirs memories of warm days spent in Tuscany and Provence. When heated under a broiler, the tangy flavor of the tapenade mingles with the ripe tomatoes and melted mozzarella to make an irresistible summer sandwich. When I make tapenade, I always like to make extra to have on hand to serve with grilled vegetables or as a spread for crostini. It can be stored in the refrigerator for up to a week in a sealed container.

TAPENADE (MAKES 1½ CUPS)

½ cup pitted Kalamata olives

¼ cup pitted Sicilian green olives

4 anchovy filets, coarsely chopped

1 clove garlic, chopped

2 tablespoons capers, rinsed and drained

2 tablespoons oil-packed tuna, drained

1 tablespoon freshly squeezed lemon juice

1 cup fresh parsley leaves

¼ cup extra-virgin olive oil

¼ cup mayonnaise

1 large-diameter baguette or country French
    loaf (not a skinny baguette), cut diagonally
    into 8 ½-inch-thick slices

2 large ripe tomatoes, such as heirloom or
    beefsteak, cut into 8 ¼-inch-thick slices

8 ounces fresh mozzarella cheese, cut into
    8 slices

1 To make the tapenade, combine the olives, anchovy filets, garlic, capers, tuna, lemon juice, and parsley in a food processor and puree until smooth. While the motor is still running, slowly drizzle in the oil in a steady stream. Add the mayonnaise and process until blended. Set aside.

2 Preheat the oven broiler. To assemble the sandwiches, spread 1 tablespoon of tapenade on each slice of bread. Top with a slice of tomato, then a slice of mozzarella. Place the sandwiches on a non-stick baking sheet and place under the broiler for a few minutes to melt the cheese. Serve immediately.

This is one of my favorite sandwiches to prepare while figs are in season. The sweetness of figs and the saltiness of ham, along with warm goat cheese, are a perfect combination.

1 sweet baguette, cut in half lengthwise

½ cup extra-virgin olive oil

4 ounces Black Forest ham, thinly sliced

8 ounces soft goat cheese

4 fresh figs, stemmed and thinly sliced lengthwise

2 tablespoons freshly squeezed lemon juice

*When the figs are ripe
all the birds want to eat.* —ANONYMOUS

1 Preheat oven to 350°F. Scoop out and discard the soft interior of the baguette halves. Brush olive oil over the cut sides of the bread. Arrange the ham evenly over the bottom half of the baguette. Spread the cheese over the ham and then top with the sliced figs. Sprinkle with lemon juice, cover with top half of the baguette, and wrap in foil, leaving a small opening at the top of the foil package.

2 Bake until the cheese is melted and the sandwich is heated through, about 15 to 20 minutes. Cut sandwich into 4 equal pieces. Serve immediately, while still warm.

TOASTED SOURDOUGH CROSTINI TOPPED WITH WHITE BEAN PURÉE AND SAUTÉED GREENS

These bite-size crostini are terrific as main-course sandwiches but work equally well as appetizers. If serving as a main course, allot four crostini per person. The blending of pureed beans, olive oil, and lemon is extremely tasty, and the garlicky sautéed greens give the recipe an extra, spicy flavor. I like to serve these sandwiches when we paint green botanicals from the garden. We use the whole plant, including the roots, as a model.

1 pound dried white beans, such as cannellini,
    soaked in water overnight and drained

Fine sea salt

¾ cup plus ½ cup extra-virgin olive oil

¼ cup fresh-squeezed lemon juice

1 tablespoon lemon zest

Freshly ground black pepper

24 slices sourdough baguette, each ½-inch thick

4 cloves garlic, chopped

6 ounces coarsely chopped mixed greens such as
    escarole, mizuna, arugula, and baby bok choy

1 To make the white bean puree: Heat the beans in 2 quarts of water in a large pot to boiling. Reduce heat, cover the pot, and simmer for 30 minutes. Add salt to taste and continue cooking for another 15 minutes or until cooked, but not mushy. Drain and let cool for at least 10 minutes.

2 Place the warm beans, ¾ cup olive oil, lemon juice, lemon zest, and pepper to taste in a food processor. Puree until smooth. Add additional salt to taste if necessary.

3 Preheat the oven to broil. Place the baguette slices on a large baking pan. Toast for about 2 minutes per side, until lightly browned.

4 To make the sautéed greens: In a large sauté pan over medium heat, heat ½ cup olive oil until it begins to shimmer. Add the chopped garlic and sauté for 30 seconds. Add the mixed greens and sauté for just a few minutes until they begin to wilt but still retain their fresh green color.

5 To assemble the crostini, spread a large spoonful of warm bean puree on each slice of baguette. Top with some of the sautéed greens and serve immediately.

Smoked Salmon Sandwiches with Radish, Cucumber, and Ginger Relish

Serves 6

This tangy relish flavored with honey, vinegar, soy sauce, and fresh ginger makes a great sandwich spread for smoked or cured salmon. You can serve the sandwiches whole or serve half a sandwich with a salad—just sprinkle a little extra-virgin olive oil and lemon juice on mixed greens with some sea salt and freshly ground black pepper.

18 red radishes, washed and trimmed

4 green onions, cut into 24 pieces

1½-inch segment of fresh ginger, peeled and minced

2 cucumbers, peeled, seeded, and cut into chunks

¼ cup rice vinegar

1 teaspoon honey

1 teaspoon low-sodium soy sauce

6 French rolls, cut in half

¾ cup mayonnaise

6 large leaves of butter lettuce

8 ounces thinly sliced smoked salmon or
    Home-Cured Salmon (page 104)

Freshly ground black pepper

1 Coarsely chop 12 of the radishes. Thinly slice the remaining radishes and reserve for garnishing.

2 In the bowl of a food processor, add the chopped radishes, the green onions, and the ginger and process until finely chopped. Add the cucumbers and pulse 15 times, until mixture is combined but still a little chunky. Set aside.

3 In a medium bowl, combine the vinegar, honey, and soy sauce and stir until the honey dissolves. Add the cucumber mixture, stir, and let stand for 15 minutes. Drain in a fine-mesh sieve, pressing to squeeze out any excess moisture. Return the radish-cucumber relish to the bowl and set aside or chill until ready to assemble the sandwiches.

4 Preheat the oven to broil. Using the tines of a fork, hollow out the cut sides of the sandwich roll bottoms slightly to create a cavity for the relish. Place both tops and bottoms of the rolls on a baking sheet, cut sides up, and broil for 3 minutes or until lightly toasted.

5 To assemble the sandwiches, spread 1 table-spoon of mayonnaise on each of the cut sides of the rolls. Spread a spoonful of cucumber relish on the bottom half of each roll. Top with a lettuce leaf and a few slices of salmon. Garnish with a few slices of radish and some freshly ground black pepper. Add the tops of the rolls and serve.

Black Peppercorns  Cardamom  Nutmeg  Cloves  Lombok chilies

 Garlic

 White Mustard Seed

Negro Chili

CURRIED CHICKEN PITA SANDWICHES WITH CARROTS AND GOLDEN RAISINS

Serves 4

I like to serve this spicy chicken salad in pita bread as a sandwich, but you can also serve it on top of salad greens. The salad gets its zing from grated orange zest, ginger, and curry powder. Carrots and raisins add just the right sweetness, and cashews give it crunch. If serving as a salad, you'll need an additional cup of salad greens to make four servings.

½ cup plus 1 tablespoon mayonnaise

1 teaspoon grated orange zest

1 tablespoon orange juice

1½ teaspoons curry powder

¾ teaspoon grated peeled fresh ginger

2½ cups diced grilled boneless, skinless
  chicken breasts (about 1 pound)

¾ cup grated carrots

¼ cup golden raisins

⅛ cup thinly sliced green onions

2 tablespoons chopped raw cashews

4 (6-inch) pita breads

3 cups salad greens

1 Combine the mayonnaise, orange zest, orange juice, curry powder, and grated ginger in a large bowl and stir until blended. Add the chicken, carrots, raisins, green onions, and cashews and toss well to combine. Cover and chill until ready to serve.

2 To serve, cut each pita in half crosswise. Gently open each half, separating the layers to make a pocket. Spoon about ¾ cup of the chicken mixture into each pocket, and add about ¾ cup of the salad greens. Place 2 sandwich halves on each of 4 serving plates and serve immediately.

Caraway

Caper Buds

 Cinnamon Sticks Sesame Seed Green Peppercorns  Saffron Threads  Juniper Berries

Allspice

Crushed Red Pepper

Fennel Seed

Star Anise

Pickling Spice

TAHINI-MARINATED CHICKEN SANDWICHES

Serves 4

I'm always looking for new ways to create unusual flavors in sandwiches. Tahini, or sesame paste, is available at most grocery stores, and makes a wonderful marinade for chicken when combined with fresh ginger and yogurt. The honey-ginger sauce enhances the flavors of the marinade, adding a piquant richness to the sandwich.

MARINADE

3 green onions, coarsely chopped

1 tablespoon minced, peeled fresh ginger

2 cloves garlic

2 tablespoons tahini

1 cup plain yogurt

2 whole boneless, skinless chicken breasts,
    split into 4 halves

1 tablespoon extra-virgin olive oil

1 teaspoon fine sea salt

½ teaspoon freshly ground black pepper

CREAMY HONEY-GINGER SAUCE

2 teaspoons extra-virgin olive oil

1 tablespoon minced, peeled fresh ginger

¼ cup chopped green onions

⅓ cup honey

½ cup plain yogurt

½ cup mayonnaise

4 French-style sandwich rolls, halved lengthwise

2 handfuls mixed salad greens

1 To prepare the chicken, place the onions, ginger, garlic, tahini, and yogurt in a food processor and process until it has a creamy consistency. Transfer to a large bowl and add the chicken breasts, coating them with the marinade. Cover and refrigerate overnight.

Heat a large skillet or grill pan over medium-high heat and add the olive oil. Remove the chicken from the marinade, scraping off the excess. Sprinkle with salt and pepper, and place the chicken in the hot pan. Cook until golden, about 5 to 7 minutes per side. Set aside to cool. Cut the chicken diagonally into ¼-inch-thick slices.

2 To make the sauce, heat the olive oil in a saucepan over medium heat. Add the ginger, green onions, and honey. Cook for 1 minute. Let cool, then stir in the yogurt and mayonnaise until blended.

3 To serve, spread some of the sauce on the bottoms of the sandwich rolls. Add the chicken slices, then the salad greens, dividing equally between the 4 sandwiches. Top with the remaining halves of the rolls. Cut sandwiches in half and serve.

Ginger

Black Sesame Seed

Pink Peppercorns

Dried Turmeric

Cumin Seeds

Guajillo Chiles

Poppy Seeds

Vanilla Bean

103

HOME-CURED SALMON WITH HORSERADISH-DILL CREAM SAUCE

Serves 6 as a main course, 12 as an appetizer

We grow herbs in our garden year-round. Feathery dill weed is one of our favorite herbs to grow, eat, and paint. It is a wonderful addition to salads and a natural flavoring for home-cured salmon and homemade pickles. This salmon recipe can easily be doubled with a larger salmon fillet to feed a crowd. We serve it on top of toasted slices of brioche slathered with tangy Horseradish-Dill Cream Sauce and garnished with capers.

¼ cup coarse sea salt

¼ cup granulated sugar

1½ teaspoons freshly ground white pepper

1½ teaspoons freshly ground black pepper

¼ cup coarsely chopped fresh dill, plus a few
    whole sprigs for garnish

¼ cup coarsely chopped fennel fronds

1 tail-end salmon fillet (1 to 1½ pounds), skin
    on and scaled

⅛ cup vodka

HORSERADISH-DILL CREAM SAUCE

2 teaspoons prepared horseradish

2 teaspoons finely grated onion

1 teaspoon Dijon mustard

1 teaspoon sugar

2 tablespoons white wine vinegar

1 tablespoon minced fresh dill

Large pinch of salt

¾ cup heavy cream

6 large slices of brioche bread from a large loaf

5-ounce jar of capers, drained, for garnish

1 Select a 2-inch-deep glass or ceramic baking dish that fits the length of the fish as closely as possible. In a small bowl, combine the salt, sugar, white and black pepper, dill, and fennel. Spread half of this mixture on the bottom of the baking dish. Lay the salmon, skin side down, in the dish. Gently rub the remaining salt mixture over the flesh side of the fillet. Slowly drizzle the vodka over the fish, being careful not to rinse off the salt mixture.

2 Place a large sheet of plastic wrap directly on top of the fish, pressing it against the fillet and sealing the wrap tightly around the sides of the dish. Place something that weighs several pounds (such as cans or bottles, on their sides) on top of the fish. Refrigerate the salmon for 2 days, turning the fish over once a day, being sure to weight down the salmon again after each turn.

(continued)

HOME-CURED SALMON WITH HORSERADISH-DILL CREAM SAUCE (CONTINUED)

3 To make the horseradish sauce, in a small bowl stir together all the ingredients except the cream. In a large bowl, whip the cream into soft peaks, and then stir in the horseradish mixture by hand. Cover with plastic wrap and chill until ready to serve.

4 When ready to serve, preheat the oven to 350°F. Toast the slices of brioche on a baking sheet for 2 minutes per side, or until lightly toasted. Remove the fish from the refrigerator. Pour off the collected juices and wipe off excess brine and dill. Transfer fish to a cutting board. With a very sharp carving knife, skin the fillet, and then cut the fish crosswise into very thin (1/8-inch-thick) slices.

5 To serve, spread a large spoonful of the horseradish-dill cream sauce on top of each slice of toast. Top with a few slices of salmon and garnish with small sprigs of fresh dill and the capers. To serve as an appetizer, slice in half. Both salmon and horseradish sauce can be stored in the refrigerator, covered tightly with plastic wrap, for up to 1 week.

Mini Pizzas with Italian Plum Tomatoes, Red Onions, and Basil

Makes 4 (7-inch) pizzas

Colorful mini pizzas make a perfect meal any time of year. You can vary the toppings according to what's available in season, but my favorite combination is ripe plum tomatoes, red onion, and fresh basil from the garden. Serve the pizzas with a simple side salad of mixed baby greens dressed with a sprinkling of olive oil, a squeeze of lemon, and a pinch of sea salt.

Pizza Dough

½ envelope active dry yeast (1¼ teaspoon)

1 tablespoon sugar

¾ cup warm (105° to 115°F) water

1¾ cups unbleached all-purpose flour

¼ cup semolina

1½ teaspoons fine sea salt

About 4 tablespoons extra-virgin olive oil for
    oiling the bowl and brushing on pizzas

2 ounces part-skim mozzarella cheese, grated

2 vine-ripened Italian plum tomatoes, peeled
    (page 151) and sliced

½ red onion, diced

4 cloves garlic, thinly sliced

¼ cup lightly packed whole fresh basil leaves

1 In a small bowl, dissolve the yeast and sugar in the warm water. Let stand until foamy, about 5 minutes.

2 Combine the flour, semolina, and sea salt either by hand or in a heavy-duty electric mixer with a bread hook, and add the yeast mixture.

Mix well until the dough is smooth. Turn the dough out onto a lightly floured surface and knead until smooth and no longer sticky. Shape into a ball and place in a lightly oiled bowl. Cover and set aside for 30 minutes or until dough has doubled in volume.

3 Punch dough down. Divide the dough into 4 equal balls. Roll out each ball to a thickness of ½ inch. Place them on a lightly floured baking sheet. Cover and set aside for 15 minutes.

4 Place a pizza stone on the center rack of the oven and preheat oven to 450°F. Meanwhile, flatten the center of each pizza with your fingers until you have a disk measuring 7 inches across, leaving a ¼-inch area around the perimeter unflattened. Brush the flattened areas with a little olive oil. Sprinkle the grated mozzarella cheese onto each pizza. Add a few slices of tomato and sprinkle with some of the diced red onion. Scatter some of the garlic slices and arrange the whole basil leaves on top. In batches, to accommodate the size and shape of your pizza stone, bake for 8 to 10 minutes on the stone or until the dough is firm and lightly browned.

FOUR-CHEESE PIZZAS WITH MIXED HERBS AND HERB FLOWERS

When we paint herbs with their flowers, recreating 19th-century botanical illustrations, I like to serve this flavorful pizza. The aroma of the herbs and their flowers takes us back to the English knot gardens of yesteryear.

1 recipe pizza dough (page 109)

¼ cup extra-virgin olive oil, divided

4 ounces shredded mozzarella cheese

4 ounces shredded fontina cheese

4 ounces shredded smoked Gouda

4 ounces Parmigiano-Reggiano cheese, grated

1 tablespoon minced fresh oregano

1 tablespoon minced fresh parsley

1 tablespoon minced fresh basil

1 tablespoon minced fresh thyme

Flowers from oregano, basil, and thyme, for garnish

1. Make the pizza dough according to the recipe for Mini Pizzas through step 3, but divide the dough into 2 equal balls. Roll out each ball to a thickness of ½ inch. Place them on a lightly floured baking sheet, cover, and set aside for 15 minutes.

2. Place a pizza stone on the center rack of the oven and preheat the oven to 450°F. Meanwhile, flatten the center of each disk of dough with your fingers until you have a circle measuring 12 inches across, leaving a ¼-inch area around the perimeter unflattened. Brush the flattened areas of each circle with 1 tablespoon of olive oil.

3. In a medium bowl mix all the cheeses together, reserving half of the Parmigiano-Reggiano for later. Sprinkle each round of dough evenly with half of the cheese mixture, then sprinkle each with half of the herbs. Drizzle evenly with the remaining olive oil.

4. Place one of the pizzas on the preheated pizza stone and bake until the crust is golden brown and puffy, about 8 to 10 minutes. Remove from the oven to a board and sprinkle with half the remaining Parmigiano-Reggiano cheese. Garnish with herb flowers and serve. Bake and finish the other pizza.

A COOK'S HERB GARDEN PLAN

The colors heralding the arrival of spring along our California coast are yellow and green. Yellow mustard flowers and daffodils, and hillsides green from winter rains are the first signs that winter is over. Our garden's asparagus bed keeps us in fresh spears from March through June. When the first spears have pushed their way above ground, we harvest them for this yellow and green frittata to serve at lunch to our painting classes. Accompanied by the Flower Petal Salad (page 61), this frittata makes a colorful main course for Easter brunch as well.

1 pound medium asparagus

1 small orange bell pepper

1 small red bell pepper

1 tablespoon butter

2 medium shallots, peeled and minced

2 scallions, green and white portions, thinly sliced

5 large eggs

¼ cup mayonnaise

1 teaspoon fine sea salt

¼ teaspoon freshly ground black pepper

2 tablespoons finely chopped Italian parsley

1 cup shelled fresh garden peas

1 Preheat oven to 350°F. Butter a 2-quart (8 by 12-inch rectangular or oval) baking dish. Snap off the tough ends of the asparagus. Peel the lower part of the asparagus stalks with a peeler.

2 Bring a large pot of water to a boil. Boil the asparagus spears for 1 minute, and then transfer them to a large bowl of ice water to stop the cooking. Drain asparagus and pat dry. Cut half of the asparagus spears into ½-inch lengths on a diagonal, reserving the remaining uncut spears for topping the frittata.

3 Cut the orange pepper lengthwise, core and seed it, and then slice it lengthwise into ¼-inch thick strips. Prepare the red pepper the same way, but cut it into small dice. In a skillet over moderate heat, melt the butter and sauté the orange and red peppers, shallots, and scallions until tender, about 10 to 12 minutes. Reserve ¼ cup of the sautéed orange pepper strips for topping the frittata.

4 In a large bowl, whisk together the eggs, mayonnaise, salt, pepper, and parsley until smooth. Stir in the sautéed pepper mixture, the cut asparagus, and the fresh peas. Pour the mixture into the prepared baking dish. Arrange the reserved asparagus spears and pepper strips on top. Bake for 35 to 45 minutes, until the egg mixture is set. Let cool for 10 minutes before serving.

SUMMER TOMATO TARTS WITH GOAT CHEESE AND MINT

Serves 8

I usually have lots of mint growing in the garden. I grow it in large wine barrels all throughout the year so that I always have fresh mint on hand. Mint is so refreshing and summery when combined with just-picked, ripe tomatoes and goat cheese in this colorful savory tart.

1 package (2 sheets, 9½ by 9½ inches) frozen
   puff pastry, thawed

8 ounces soft goat cheese

4 to 6 large ripe Roma tomatoes, sliced lengthwise
   into ¼-inch-thick slices

4 tablespoons extra-virgin olive oil

8 tablespoons sliced fresh mint leaves

2 ounces Parmigiano-Reggiano cheese, shaved
   with a cheese slicer or vegetable peeler

Fine sea salt

1 Preheat an oven to 425°F. Line two baking pans with parchment paper.

2 Using a sharp knife, cut each sheet of puff pastry into 4 equal squares. Place the pastry squares on the prepared baking pans and refrigerate the pans for 15 minutes.

3 Remove the baking pans from the refrigerator. Using the point of a sharp knife, lightly score a border ¼-inch in from the edge of each pastry square. Prick the centers of the squares with the tines of a fork.

4 Divide the goat cheese into 8 equal parts with a knife. Spread one portion of goat cheese onto each pastry square, staying inside the scored edge. Place 3 to 4 slices of tomato in the center of each tart. Using a pastry brush, coat the tomatoes with a little olive oil and sprinkle each tart with a tablespoon of mint leaves. Lay a few shavings of Parmigiano-Reggiano cheese across each tart and sprinkle with a little sea salt.

5 Bake the tarts in the preheated oven for 15 to 20 minutes, or until the pastry is golden brown. Serve on individual plates while still warm.

Early Girl

Italian Costoluto

Purple Calabash

Green Bell Pepper

Elberta Girl

*Dirty hands, iced tea, garden fragrances thick in the air
and a blanket of color before me, who could ask for more?* —BEV ADAMS

THE SUMMER GARDEN

ummer is filled with creative classes based on painting from the garden. Roses begin to bloom in June. And there is an abundance of flowers, herbs, and vegetables growing in the garden that I bring into the studio for my students to paint. This is also the time of the year when I teach students to paint bird eggs, shells, seaweed, butterflies, and insects. Our garden is producing a colorful palette of organic vegetables, greens, and flowers for our lunches, and I prepare my favorite warm-weather foods—lots of chilled soups, salads, and sandwiches bursting with flavor. What's in season inspires our lunch menus. Sometimes the weather cooperates and we have tomatoes in the summer; if not, we buy them from our local farmers market until ours ripen in fall. Being near the coast, I often add shellfish to our salads and smoked or home-cured salmon to sandwiches. Herbs and herb flowers heighten the flavor of every soup, salad, tart, and pizza. Sweet-scented flowers garnish icy sorbets while rose petals and other delicate flowers flavor ice cream and flower petal salads.

In autumn, just as soon as the mushrooms start popping up throughout our woods and the cool, crisp air is filled with chimney smoke from aged oak, I notice mushroom foragers with baskets or burlap sacks scurrying around the woods looking for their favorite wild mushrooms. Our town celebrates the arrival of mushroom season with an annual mushroom festival.

Mushrooms are always favorite botanical subjects in my painting classes. We study books of botanical styles of the Old Masters for inspiration and students are served this mushroom tart filled with smoky mozzarella and Parmigiano-Reggiano cheeses for our class lunch. My daughter Sunny artfully arranges woodsy mushrooms and fennel fronds from the garden on the surface of the tart to resemble an antique botanical print, a case of life imitating art.

To create your own botanical mushroom tart, practice arranging your pan-browned mushrooms on a paper towel cut to the same size as your tart pan. Add fennel fronds in between the mushrooms until you find an arrangement that you like. Transfer your design to the partially baked tart and return it to the oven.

PASTRY

1½ cups unbleached all-purpose flour

¾ teaspoon fine sea salt

½ cup (4 ounces/1 stick) cold unsalted butter,
    cut into small pieces

3 to 4 tablespoons ice water

FILLING

4 eggs

¾ cup heavy cream

2 cups shredded smoked mozzarella cheese

1 cup grated Parmigiano-Reggiano cheese

4 ounces assorted fresh wild mushrooms
    (such as shiitake, chanterelle, and nameko)

Extra-virgin olive oil for brushing

Several sprigs of fresh fennel fronds

1 To make the pastry dough: Process the flour and salt in a food processor until combined. Add the butter and process until mixture resembles coarse meal, about 10 seconds. With the processor running, pour the ice water through the feed tube in a thin, steady stream and process just until the dough begins to hold together. Remove the dough from the food processor, wrap in plastic wrap, and refrigerate for at least an hour.

2 Preheat oven to 350°F. Turn the dough out onto a lightly floured work surface and roll it into a 10 by 13-inch rectangle, ½-inch thick. Gently lay the dough into an 8 by 11-inch rectangular tart pan with removable bottom, pressing the dough into the bottom and up the sides. Run a rolling pin across the top of the pan to trim off excess dough. Place the tart pan in the freezer and chill for

(continued)

10 minutes. Remove from the freezer and prick the bottom of the tart shell all over with a fork. Line the shell with parchment paper or aluminum foil and weight it with dried beans or pie weights. Bake for 20 minutes. Remove the beans and foil or paper, and return to oven for 10 minutes. Remove from oven and set aside to cool.

3 To make the filling: Whisk the eggs and cream together and stir in the cheeses. Pour into the cooled tart shell and return to the oven. Bake for 20 minutes, until almost set.

4 Meanwhile, slice the chanterelles and some of the shiitakes in half lengthwise and brush with a little olive oil. Heat a skillet on the stovetop over high heat and cook all the mushrooms

except namekos for 4 to 5 minutes, or until the edges start to brown slightly. Gently transfer the mushrooms to a plate.

5 After removing the tart from the oven, carefully arrange the mushrooms and fennel fronds on top to resemble a botanical print. Return the tart to the oven and bake for 10 minutes longer, until the filling is fully set and golden. Remove from oven and cool on a rack for 5 minutes, then cut into equal portions and serve.

1. Morel   2. Velvet Pioppini   3. Chanterelle   4. Tree Oyster   5. White Button   6. Royal Trumpet   7. Horn of Plenty
8. Shiitake

SWEETS

ROSE PETAL ICE CREAM   124

ROSE PETAL SYRUP   127

MEYER LEMON ICE   128

CHOCOLATE CHUNK COOKIES   133

DARK CHOCOLATE AND
    ORANGE PISTACHIO COOKIES   134

SAND DOLLAR COOKIES   137

STRAWBERRY TARTLETS   138

RHUBARB-STRAWBERRY CRUMBLE   143

CITRUS-OLIVE OIL CAKE   144

WHITE FIGS WITH HONEY, RUM,
    AND WHIPPED CREAM   145

POACHED APPLES STUFFED WITH BRIE,
    WITH CHAMPAGNE SABAYON   148

ROSE PETAL ICE CREAM

Makes 1 quart; serves 6

Homemade ice cream is one of my favorite desserts and I enjoy serving it to my painting classes because I can make it several days ahead of time. In late spring, when I host classes on painting flowers, I like to serve this delicately flavored rose petal ice cream to celebrate the first bloom of my garden roses. It is flavored with homemade rose petal syrup and garnished with rose petals picked the morning of class. If you don't have access to unsprayed roses for the syrup, you can buy rose-flavored syrup, such as Monin brand, instead. Garnish the ice cream with other unsprayed edible flower petals or a sprig of mint.

1½ cups heavy cream

1 cup whole milk

⅔ cup superfine sugar

¼ cup Rose Petal Syrup, plus
　　more for drizzling (page 127)

½ vanilla bean, split lengthwise

¼ cup unsprayed rose petals
　　for garnish

1 In a medium saucepan, combine the cream, milk, and sugar. Cook over medium heat, stirring until sugar is dissolved, and then continue to cook for about 3 to 4 minutes until tiny bubbles form around the edges of the pan; do not bring to a boil. Remove from heat. Stir in the rose syrup and the vanilla bean, scraping the vanilla bean's seeds into the mixture. Cover with plastic wrap and let stand for 30 minutes. Refrigerate for at least 2½ hours, or until thoroughly chilled.

2 Remove the vanilla pod and transfer the mixture to an ice cream maker. Freeze according to the manufacturer's instructions.

3 To serve, place a scoop of ice cream in each bowl, drizzle with ½ teaspoon of rose syrup, and top with a few fresh rose petals.

ROSE PETAL SYRUP

In May and June when my garden roses first bloom, I make rose petal syrup to flavor a delicately aromatic rose petal ice cream. For a lovely pastel-colored apéritif, try adding a spoonful to a glass of sparkling wine, or drizzle it over aged cheese for dessert.

6 ounces fresh, fragrant rose petals (pink or red),
    12 petals reserved

7 cups sugar

Juice of one lemon, including the seeds and pulp

The garden is a love song, a duet between a human being and Mother Nature. —Jeff Cox

1 Pick the rose petals from unsprayed roses in the morning when they are most fragrant. Grasp the tips of the rose and with scissors cut through all the petals near the center, removing only the colored part of the petals, not the white tip at the base of the flower. Place the petals in a glass bowl and toss with 1¾ cups of sugar. Coat well, squeezing the petals to bruise slightly. Cover with plastic wrap and let stand in a cool place overnight.

2 The next day, in a large saucepan, combine 3½ cups water and the remaining 5¼ cups sugar. Bring to a boil, stirring, until the sugar dissolves. Add the lemon juice and the macerated rose petals with their sugary liquid to the pan and return to a boil.

3 Reduce to a high simmer and cook for 30 minutes, until a candy thermometer reads 212°F. Remove from the heat and let cool to room temperature. Strain, removing the rose petals and lemon seeds. Pour into sterilized bottles. Add 3 of the reserved fresh rose petals for decoration to each bottle. Store in refrigerator.

Meyer Lemon Ice

Meyer lemons grow well in my garden and throughout northern California. They are my favorite lemons to use in desserts because they are sweet and contain less acid than other lemons, and the zest from the peel adds a delicious perfume to any recipe. If Meyer lemons aren't available, use the Eureka or Lisbon varieties commonly available in markets year-round. This simple, refreshing ice is sorbet-like in texture and doesn't require an ice cream maker.

I save the empty lemon shells to wash my hands with after gardening or painting. Rubbing the inside of the skin against my fingertips always helps with the dryness that occurs when working with garden soil. It also cleans away paint stains on hands after a day of painting in the studio.

2 cups fresh Meyer lemon juice, strained (from about 18 medium-size lemons), plus finely-grated zest from 3 lemons (tip: zest lemons first, right into the baking dish)

2 cups water

2 cups granulated sugar

Small sprigs of mint or lemon balm, edible flowers, or small berries, optional

1 Zest three lemons right into an 8-inch Pyrex baking dish. Juice all of the lemons to get 2 cups of juice. Combine the lemon juice with the water in a small saucepan. Stir in the sugar. Set over moderate heat and bring to a boil, stirring constantly until the sugar is dissolved. Remove from heat and cool to room temperature.

2 Pour the lemon mixture into an 8-inch square Pyrex baking dish and stir well to combine with the lemon zest. Cover dish with plastic wrap and place it in the freezer. Let it freeze for 6 hours or overnight. After about 3 hours, stir the mixture to ensure that the zest is well incorporated into the ice.

3 To serve, remove the pan of lemon ice from the freezer 20 minutes before serving to allow it to soften slightly. Using an ice cream scoop (run the metal scoop under hot water if necessary), scoop individual balls and place one in each bowl. Top with a sprig of the herbs and flowers or berries.

EDIBLE FLOWERS

I like to think of edible flowers as my culinary paint box when creating dishes for my family and students. Adding flowers not only creates a variety of delicate flavors, the blossoms also add splashes of color, giving dishes a more painterly quality. When I started my garden, I chose flowers that I especially wanted to paint, but over time I have included more flowers and herbs for use in cooking as well. Here are some of my favorites:

Arugula	Lavender
Basil	Lilac
Bee Balm	Mint
Borage	Nasturtium
Calendula	Pansy
Carnation	Rose
Chamomile	Rosemary
Chives	Sage
Citrus (lemon)	Scented Geranium
Cornflower	Sunflower
Dill	Thyme
Fennel	Violet
Johnny-Jump-Up	Zucchini

CHOCOLATE CHUNK COOKIES

This recipe was inspired by my friend Gayle Ortiz. She is not only a talented artist and cook, but she also owns a popular bakery and rosticceria in the nearby town of Capitola. Like Gayle, I use a good quality chocolate like Green & Black's Organic Baking Chocolate with 72% cocoa to make these irresistible chunky cookies.

½ cup (4 ounces/1 stick) unsalted butter, softened

½ cup packed dark brown sugar

½ cup granulated sugar

1 egg, lightly beaten

1 tablespoon milk

1 teaspoon vanilla extract

1 cup unbleached all-purpose flour, sifted

½ teaspoon baking powder

½ teaspoon baking soda

½ teaspoon salt

1 cup quick-cooking oats

8 ounces dark baking chocolate, chopped into
¼-inch chunks

½ cup coarsely chopped walnuts

1 In a large mixing bowl using an electric mixer, cream the butter and both sugars until light and fluffy. Add the egg, milk, and vanilla and beat until blended.

2 In a medium bowl, sift the flour, baking powder, baking soda, and salt together. Add to the butter mixture and mix just until blended. Stir in the oats, chocolate, and walnuts.

3 Cover with plastic wrap and refrigerate the dough for one hour.

4 Preheat an oven to 350°F. Line cookie pans with parchment paper.

5 Remove the dough from the refrigerator and shape dough by tablespoonfuls into balls. Place the balls 3 inches apart on the cookie pans and flatten slightly. Bake until the edges are slightly browned, 8 to 12 minutes.

6 Remove from the oven and let cool on the pans for 5 minutes. Transfer cookies to wire racks to cool completely. Store for up to 2 weeks in an airtight cookie tin.

LEFT: Chocolate Chunk Cookies and
Dark Chocolate and Orange Pistachio Cookies

DARK CHOCOLATE AND ORANGE PISTACHIO COOKIES   Makes about 5 dozen cookies

Chocolate pairs well with a variety of flavors. For these Middle Eastern-inspired cookies, I've paired rich dark chocolate with the flavors of oranges and pistachios. They are always a hit with my students!

1 cup unbleached all-purpose flour

1 cup shelled pistachio nuts, finely ground in
   a spice or coffee mill

½ cup (4 ounces/1 stick) unsalted butter

⅓ cup maple syrup

2 tablespoons frozen orange juice concentrate

1 tablespoon finely grated orange zest (from
   2 medium oranges)

⅔ cup packed light brown sugar

5 to 6 ounces dark baking chocolate, preferably
   72% cocoa, finely chopped

The hum of bees is the voice of the garden.

—ELIZABETH LAWRENCE

1 Preheat oven to 375°F. Line 2 cookie pans with parchment paper.

2 Mix the flour and ground nuts together in a medium bowl until blended and set aside. In a medium saucepan over medium heat, heat the butter, maple syrup, orange juice concentrate, orange zest, and sugar to boiling. Remove the pan from the heat and gradually stir in the flour and nut mixture. Let cool to room temperature and then stir in the chopped chocolate. The dough will be stiff.

3 Drop rounded teaspoonfuls of the dough 3 inches apart on the parchment-lined pans. Bake cookies about 10 to 11 minutes.

4 Remove pans from the oven and let cookies cool on the pans for 5 minutes. Transfer cookies to wire racks to cool completely. Repeat with remaining dough when pans are cool. Store for up to 2 weeks in an airtight cookie tin.

SAND DOLLAR COOKIES

I like to serve these cookies when I give classes in painting shells. I score the top of each cookie with a five-legged star to resemble a sand dollar. They get their sandy appearance from the sugar topping.

½ cup (4 ounces/1 stick) unsalted butter, softened

1 cup granulated sugar, plus 3 tablespoons for sprinkling

1 egg

1¾ cup flour

¼ teaspoon salt

1 egg white

1 Preheat oven to 325°F. Line 2 baking pans with sheets of parchment paper.

2 In a large mixing bowl using an electric mixer, beat the butter and 1 cup sugar until smooth and blended. Add the egg and continue beating until light and creamy.

3 In a small bowl, stir together the flour and salt. Add them to the butter and egg mixture, beating well to form a smooth dough.

4 Place the dough onto a lightly floured work surface. Using a rolling pin, roll the dough ⅛-inch thick. Cut the dough into rounds with a 2½-inch cookie cutter and place the rounds about 1 inch apart on the prepared pans. Gather up the scraps, reroll them, and cut into more cookies to use up all the dough. Chill the cookies on their baking pans in the refrigerator for 30 minutes before baking.

5 In a small bowl, whisk the egg white with 1 tablespoon water. Remove the chilled cookie pans from the refrigerator. Using the blunt edge of a butter knife, lightly press a five-legged star design onto each cookie round. Using a pastry brush, brush a little of the egg mixture lightly over the cookies. Sprinkle the reserved sugar over the tops.

6 Bake for about 8 to 10 minutes, or until the cookie tops have a sheen and the edges are just slightly browned. Remove from the oven and transfer cookies to racks to cool.

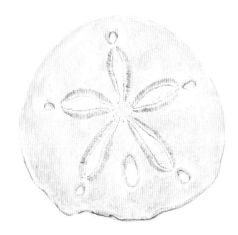

STRAWBERRY TARTLETS

Makes 12 (3-inch) tartlets; serves 6

When we paint strawberries, I gather the berries from the garden along with some of the leaves and blossoms. We grow plump strawberries and also have several Alpine strawberry plants, which bear smaller fruit with an intense fragrance and flavor. Our soil is perfect for growing these beautiful, little berries. I mulch the plants with pine needles that I gather from the base of our large Ponderosa pine tree. Berries love pine or oak mulch at their feet; it keeps their soil acidic, cool, and moist.

These tartlets are simple to make and the pastry shells can be prepared up to two days ahead. If you don't have 12 little tartlet pans, use the number you have and make the tartlet shells in batches. I like to serve two tartlets per person.

PASTRY

1½ cups unbleached all-purpose flour

½ teaspoon salt

Pinch of sugar

5½ tablespoons unsalted butter, chilled and cut
    into cubes

3 tablespoons vegetable shortening, chilled

¼ cup ice water

FILLING

¾ cup strawberry jam or preserves

1 cup heavy whipping cream

12 strawberries (approximately ½ pound),
    stemmed and hulled

1 Sift flour, salt, and sugar together in a bowl. Add the butter and shortening and cut them into the dry ingredients with a pastry blender or 2 knives until the mixture resembles coarse meal. Sprinkle the ice water over the dough and blend it in to make a workable dough, mixing lightly with a fork.

2 Turn the dough out onto a lightly floured work surface and, using the heel of your hands, spread the dough away from you several times. Scrape up the smeared dough into a ball, wrap with plastic wrap, and refrigerate for 2 hours.

3 Unwrap the dough, place it on a lightly floured surface, and pound it a few times with a rolling pin to soften it. Roll it out to ⅛ inch thick. Line 12 (3-inch) tart pans with the dough, pat dough into place, and trim off excess dough, pressing dough against the edges of the pans. Refrigerate for 30 minutes.

(continued)

Strawberry Tartlets (continued)

4 Preheat oven to 400°F. Remove chilled tartlets from the refrigerator and prick the dough on the base and sides with a fork. Line each tart pan with a piece of foil and fill with dried beans or pastry weights. Bake for 10 minutes, just until the dough is beginning to turn golden. Remove from oven. Remove weights and foil, and then continue to bake tartlets until golden brown, 10 to 12 minutes more. Let cool on a wire rack. Finally, remove cooled tart shells from pans. If not using right away, tart shells can be stored for up to 2 days in the refrigerator in a sealed container.

5 Spoon the strawberry jam or preserves into a small saucepan and heat over low heat for 7 to 10 minutes. Do not boil. Strain the mixture through a fine sieve into a small bowl to separate the strawberry syrup from the pulp. Add 2 tablespoons of hot water to the syrup to thin it slightly. Let cool. Reserve the strawberry pulp in another bowl and let it cool.

6 In a large bowl, whip the cream to stiff peaks using a whisk or electric mixer. To assemble the tartlets, spread each cooled tartlet shell with 2 teaspoons of the reserved strawberry pulp. Spoon a dollop of whipped cream over the filling in each tartlet. Place one strawberry atop the cream. Drizzle 1 tablespoon of the reserved strawberry syrup over each tartlet. Chill the tartlets in the refrigerator until ready to serve.

Rhubarb-Strawberry Crumble

In early spring, I watch our rhubarb plants send their large green leaves on bright pink stalks out of the soil, and wait for the right time to harvest so I can make this wonderful, sweet-tart dessert. I like the tartness of rhubarb with the natural sweetness of the strawberries, and not too much added sugar. The stalks are the only edible part of the plant, but the leaves are lovely to paint. If I'm lucky, I sometimes catch a glimpse of a bird taking a bath in the rainwater that accumulates in those large leaves.

1½ pounds rhubarb, trimmed and cut into ½-inch
    dice, about 5 cups

2 cups (about 10 ounces) hulled, sliced strawberries

½ cup granulated sugar

2 tablespoons all-purpose flour

Juice of ½ lemon

1 teaspoon vanilla extract

Topping

½ cup rolled oats

½ cup all-purpose flour

½ cup packed light brown sugar

2 tablespoons butter, at room temperature

1 teaspoon ground cinnamon

½ cup slivered almonds

Fine sea salt

2 tablespoons apple juice

1 pint vanilla ice cream or frozen yogurt, optional

1 Preheat oven to 375°F. In a large bowl, toss together rhubarb, strawberries, granulated sugar, flour, lemon juice, and vanilla. Transfer the mixture to a shallow 1½ quart baking dish or a deep 9-inch pie plate, distributing the fruit evenly.

2 Combine oats, flour, brown sugar, butter, and cinnamon in a bowl; with a fork or your hands, work the ingredients together until the mixture is crumbly. Stir in the almonds and a pinch of salt. Add apple juice and stir until mixture is evenly moistened. Spread the topping evenly over the fruit. Bake for 35 to 45 minutes, or until fruit is bubbling and the topping is golden. Serve with a scoop of vanilla ice cream or frozen yogurt if desired.

CITRUS-OLIVE OIL CAKE

This homey, rustic cake is best served when it's made a day or so ahead. This allows the flavors of the citrus fruit and olive oil to mingle into a moist sweet-and-tangy cake. You can serve it as is or with a dusting of confectioners' sugar. I like to garnish the serving plate with a garland of orange slices or little sprigs of olive branches.

2 small juice oranges

1 lemon

1 cup all-purpose flour

1 tablespoon baking powder

4 eggs, at room temperature

½ teaspoon salt

1½ cups granulated sugar

1½ cups (6 ounces) almonds, toasted (page 151) and finely ground to a coarse powder in a spice mill or food processor

⅔ cup extra-virgin olive oil

Confectioners' sugar for dusting

1 Put the oranges and lemon in a large saucepan and add water to cover. Bring to a simmer and cook, uncovered, for 30 minutes. Drain the fruit and let cool to the touch.

2 Cut the lemon in half and discard the pulp and seeds. Cut the oranges in half and discard the seeds, but reserve the pulp. Put the lemon rinds and orange halves in a food processor and chop finely. Set aside.

3 Preheat the oven to 350°F. Sift the flour and baking powder together into a medium bowl and set aside. In a large bowl using a whisk or electric mixer, combine the eggs and salt and beat until foamy. Gradually beat in the sugar. Using a rubber spatula, gently fold in the flour mixture and then the chopped citrus, pulverized almonds, and olive oil just until incorporated. Do not overmix.

4 Pour the batter into an ungreased 10-inch springform pan with removable bottom. Bake for about 1 hour and 15 minutes, or until the center of the cake is set and a toothpick inserted in the center comes out clean. Let cool completely in the pan on a wire rack, then unmold from the pan and invert onto a serving plate, topside up. Dust the top with confectioners' sugar and serve.

144

White Figs with Honey, Rum, and Whipped Cream

Serves 4

We love painting all the varieties of figs. Brown Turkey figs have a lovely reddish-violet-burgundy color with bright green. The Black Mission figs are dark and mysterious. And the white figs are such a lovely, fresh, leaf-green color. My daughter Wendy brings us these figs at the end of summer from her lush white fig tree, which is abundant with these beautiful fruits. White figs are larger and less sweet than dark figs. If only dark figs are available, allow 3 figs per serving and reduce the amount of honey you use to 1 tablespoon per serving.

8 white figs
8 tablespoons of honey
White rum for drizzling (optional)
1 cup heavy whipping cream

1 Cut top quarter off figs and discard. Take a spoon and press lightly on the cut top of the figs to form a hollow. Arrange all the figs in a small bowl so that the figs sit upright. Pour a tablespoon of honey into the hollow of each fig. Drizzle with rum, and chill in the refrigerator for 2 hours.

2 Whip the cream until stiff peaks form. Transfer 2 figs onto each of 4 small dessert plates. Put a large spoonful of whipped cream on each. Spoon liquid from bowl around figs on plate.

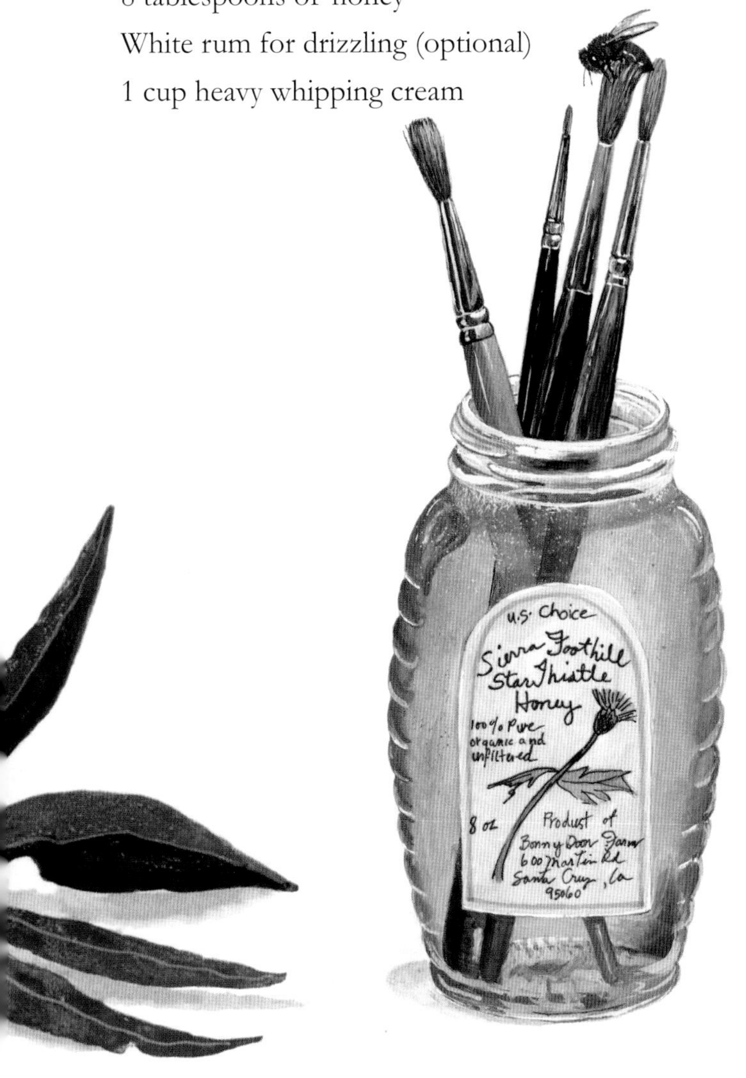

THE FALL GARDEN

Thick-Footed Morel

Our garden gives us all it can give in fall. We gather bushels of tomatoes, zucchini, carrots, and beans. Our berry bushes and old Golden Delicious apple tree are covered with fruit. If we don't harvest them quickly, the birds and squirrels eat them overnight. Our dwarf fig and pear trees in wine barrel planters bear beautiful fruit for desserts and salads, but they are also favorite subjects for painting because of their colors. As the leaves turn, we pick them to paint from too. I begin making warm savory tarts, sandwiches with melted cheese, and hearty vegetable soups for class lunches. In November, our local mushrooms start popping up. We find morels and flavorful porcini near our Monterey pines, and golden chanterelles grow around our oak trees. Painting mushroom botanicals or in a forest setting are among our favorite projects. I gather moss, lichen, leaves, and soil from our woods to recreate the forest floor in little pans for each student to paint, adding mushrooms, twigs, and sometimes a nest.

147

POACHED APPLES STUFFED WITH BRIE, WITH CHAMPAGNE SABAYON   Serves 6

When I'm in the mood for an elegant dessert, I love to make this simple recipe in the fall when my Golden Delicious apples are ripe. The Champagne sabayon is a light, creamy sauce that's the perfect complement to sweet wine-poached apples. You can use any firm apple, like Ambrosias, Pippins, or Jonathans, but do not use a baking apple such as Granny Smith, Rome, or McIntosh, as they will not retain their shape when poached.

1 (750-milliliter) bottle sweet white wine, such as Riesling or Gewurztraminer

1 cup granulated sugar

Zest of 1 lemon, peeled with a vegetable peeler

3 tablespoons freshly squeezed lemon juice (from 2 small lemons)

1 stick cinnamon

6 Golden Delicious apples, whole, peeled, with stems left on

CHAMPAGNE SABAYON

4 egg yolks at room temperature

⅓ cup granulated sugar

¾ cup Champagne

2 tablespoons kirsch

6 ounces Brie

1 In a large, deep saucepan combine the white wine, 2 cups water, sugar, lemon zest, lemon juice, and cinnamon. Bring to a boil over medium-high heat and place the apples into the liquid. Return to a boil and then reduce the heat to medium-low and poach the apples, uncovered, for 20 minutes, turning them in the liquid periodically with a spoon. Remove the pan from the heat and let apples cool completely in the poaching liquid.

2 While the apples are cooling, make the sabayon. In a large metal bowl, whisk the egg yolks and sugar to blend. Place the bowl over a saucepan of (but not touching) boiling water on the stove and continue whisking until foamy. Add the Champagne and kirsch, whisking constantly until the sauce thickens and coats the back of a spoon, about 10 minutes. Remove bowl from over the saucepan of water.

3 To serve, remove the cooled apples from the poaching liquid and core them from the bottom with an apple corer or paring knife, leaving the tops with stems intact. Slice the Brie into six long pieces and stuff the hollow of each apple with a piece of Brie. Place each apple on a dessert plate, stem up, and spoon the sabayon in a pool around the apples.

All good things which exist are the fruits of originality. —JOHN STUART MILL

BASICS

ORANGE CHAMPAGNE VINEGAR

Makes 1²/₃ cups

This vinegar recipe is inspired by the delicious Orange Muscat Champagne Vinegar from Trader Joe's markets. Use the best quality champagne vinegar you can find. I like the champagne vinegar produced by B.R. Cohn Olive Oil Co. of Glen Ellen, California. It is a true champagne vinegar made from sparkling wine that is drawn from bottles, put into oak barrels, and aged, producing a superior vinegar. You can use my Orange Champagne Vinegar in salad dressings, as a marinade for chicken or shrimp before grilling, or combined with toasted sesame oil in Asian dishes.

¾ cup champagne vinegar (from a standard
    6.7 ounce bottle)
Juice and zest of 2 oranges
¼ cup pure maple syrup
1 teaspoon angostura aromatic bitters
½ teaspoon orange extract

Combine all ingredients in a jar, top with a lid, and shake. Store in the refrigerator for up to 1 week.

Peeling and Segmenting Citrus

Using a sharp knife, cut off the peel at the top and bottom of the fruit down to the flesh. Stand the fruit on end and following the curve of the fruit, cut off the peel and white pith in strips down to the flesh. Remove any remaining bits of pith from the flesh. Cut vertically along the sectional membranes to free the segments into a bowl and discard the membranes when all the segments have been removed.

Roasting and Peeling Bell Peppers

Using tongs, place whole peppers directly over a high flame on a gas stovetop. If you do not have a gas stove, use a grill or put the peppers on a rimmed baking pan under your broiler. Turn the peppers frequently until blackened all over. Place them in a brown paper bag, folding over the top to seal, to steam and cool down for about 10 to 15 minutes. Peel the peppers by scraping the blackened skin off with a sharp knife. Remove the stem, seeds, and white ribs before cutting as directed in the recipe.

Peeling and Seeding Tomatoes

Bring a large pot of water to a boil. While the water is heating, cut out the core from each tomato with a paring knife. Drop the tomatoes into the boiling water for 30 seconds; using a wire skimmer or slotted spoon, immediately transfer the tomatoes to ice water to stop the cooking and release the skins. The peel will slip off in your hands. To seed, cut the tomatoes in half crosswise, invert each half over the sink, and squeeze out the seeds.

Toasting Nuts

Heat oven to 350°F. Place the nuts on a rimmed baking pan and toast until golden brown and aromatic. Watch the pan closely as nuts burn easily. Pine nuts will take about 5 minutes; almonds, walnuts, pistachios, pecans, and macadamia nuts take about 10 minutes. Store any unused nuts in a tightly closed container in the refrigerator for up to 6 weeks.

CANDIED WALNUTS

Candied nuts are easy to make and a nice addition to salads that include fruit and cheese. This recipe calls for walnuts but pecans are delicious as well.

1½ cups walnut halves

2 tablespoons maple syrup

1 teaspoon brown sugar

1 tablespoon butter

3 tablespoons sugar

1½ teaspoons cinnamon

Heat oven to 375°F. On a rimmed baking sheet, spread walnut halves in a single layer. Bake for 10 minutes, keeping an eye on them so they don't burn. Meanwhile, butter a large sheet of aluminum foil.

Combine maple syrup, brown sugar, and butter in a small saucepan over medium-high heat. Bring mixture to a boil, stir in the toasted walnuts, and cook, stirring constantly, for 1 minute.

Combine the sugar and cinnamon in a medium bowl. Transfer the walnuts to the sugar-spice mixture, stir well to coat the nuts, and then spread them out on the aluminum foil to cool. Store in a tightly covered tin or covered glass container for up to 3 weeks, or in the refrigerator for 6 weeks.

POACHING AND CLEANING PRAWNS

Bring 2 quarts of water to a boil in a deep saucepan or pot. Add 2 tablespoons of salt and add 1 pound of large, unshelled prawns. Boil for 2 minutes and drain in a colander. Rinse briefly under cold running water to stop the cooking, and then drain.

If the prawns have heads, twist them off and discard. Pinch the ends of the tails off with your thumbnail and index finger, and then peel the shells and feelers from the bodies. Reserve the shells in a sealable plastic bag and freeze for seafood stock, if desired, or discard.

Using a small, sharp paring knife, slide the blade down the curved back of the prawn, making a shallow slit to expose the dark vein of the prawn's intestinal tract. Holding the prawn in one hand, run the thumbnail of your other hand along the slit to remove the vein and rinse the prawn under cold running water if necessary. Drain the cleaned prawns well, place in a bowl and cover with plastic wrap, and chill in the refrigerator until ready to use. Prawns can be prepared up to 1 day ahead and refrigerated, covered tightly.

ACKNOWLEDGMENTS

My deepest gratitude extends to the following individuals who have made this book a joy to create:

Jennifer Barry, for her guidance throughout this project, and for sharing some of her favorite recipes. For her art direction and for her lovely sense of design that fills these pages, blending this book like a fine-tuned recipe, I am forever grateful.

Wendy Candelaria, whose lovely photographs enhance every page, and whose help on this project has a special place in my heart, for it was her encouragement that put the spark into this project.

Jonathan Koch, for his exquisite, passionate paintings that adorn these pages.

Eve Lynch, our managing editor, whose tireless work on this project is so appreciated and will not be forgotten.

Kristen Hall, for her technical skill and creative assistance.

Laura Belt, for supplying our studio with treasures from nature. On behalf of my students, we are so grateful.

All of our recipe testers, whose input and taste buds were an important part of this book. Thank you, Sherry Cosseboom, Annette (Annabelle) Moeller, Lisa Ford, Carlyn Clause, Wendy Candelaria, Kristen Hall, Liz Downing, Toni Jones, Blake Hallanan, Lynda Balslev, Terri Fellers, Val Igler, and Emmilea O'Toole.

Gayle Ortiz, of Gayle's Bakery and Rosticceria in Capitola, California, for her lovely foreword, and for her breads and pastries that are so often a wonderful addition to our lunches, bringing oohs and aahs from her artist fans.

A special thanks to my family, Sunny Koch, Jonathan Koch, Deorie Koch, Wendy Candelaria, Ken Candelaria, Olivia Candelaria, Catherine Candelaria, Diane Meehan, Gary Meehan, Annette Moeller, Mary Graff, Lisa Ford, and Jane Driscoll, for all their help and taste-testing. And to my two corgis, Hopper and Gingi, who taste-tested everything that dropped on the floor.

My publisher, Kirsty Melville, and editor Chris Schillig, both of Andrews McMeel, for believing in this project; I am forever thankful.

A special thank you to my students, for it was you who planted the seed that made this project grow and bloom.

Resources

Art:

Daniel Smith Art Supplies

danielsmith.com

*Excellent brushes and all art supplies,
including Winsor & Newton watercolors
and M. Graham oil paints*

Paper Source

paper-source.com

Stores nationwide

888-PAPER-11

Decorative papers, ribbons, and journals

Utrecht Art Supplies

utrechtart.com

Stores nationwide

Art supplies

Cooking:

Asaro

unitedoliveoil.com

*Agrumati Extra-Virgin Olive Oil with
Sicilian Lemon*

B. R. Cohn Winery & Olive Oil Company

brcohn.com

Champagne vinegar

Cadia Foods

mycadia.com

Organic Italian Extra-Virgin Olive Oil

Dickson Ranch Napa, California

dicksonnaparanch.com

Regina Extra-Virgin Olive Oil

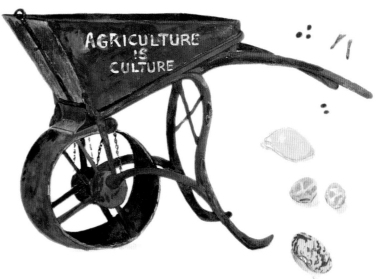

HimalaSalt

sustainablesourcing.com

Himalayan Sea Salt

Napa Valley Naturals

napavalleynaturals.com

Grand Reserve Balsamic Vinegar

Sierra Nevada Brewing Company

sierranevada.com

Pale Ale Honey Spice Mustard

Spectrum Organics

spectrumorganics.com

Organic Omega 3 Mayonnaise with Flax Oil

Trader Joe's Markets

traderjoes.com

Orange Muscat Champagne Vinegar

GARDEN:

Baker Creek Heirloom Seeds

rareseeds.com

Unusual rare heirloom seeds

Renee's Garden Seeds

reneesgarden.com

6116 Highway 9

Felton, CA 95018

Garden seeds and supplies

INDEX

A

Almonds
  Citrus–Olive Oil Cake, 144
  Grilled Chicken Sandwiches
    with Smoked Almonds
    and Dried Apricots, 94
  Mixed Greens and
    Strawberry Salad with
    Almonds and Creamy
    Orange Dressing, 46
  toasting, 151
Apples
  Butternut Squash–Apple
    Soup, 39
  Poached Apples
    Stuffed with Brie, with
    Champagne Sabayon, 148
Apricots, Dried, Grilled
    Chicken Sandwiches with
    Smoked Almonds and, 94
Art classes, 12–14, 17
Arugula
  Crispy Bacon, Arugula,
    Tomato, and Cream
    Cheese Sandwiches, 93
  Prawn, Mango, Melon,
    and Cucumber Salad
    with Lemon Vinaigrette,
    74–76
Asparagus Frittata, Spring,
    with Peas and Peppers, 113
Avocado
  Avocado-Lime Dressing, 85
  Cucumber-Avocado Soup, 29

B

Bacon
  Crispy Bacon, Arugula,
    Tomato, and Cream
    Cheese Sandwiches, 93
  Summer Squash and Fresh
    Corn Chowder, 32

Bean Purée, White, Toasted
    Sourdough Crostini Topped
    with Sautéed Greens and, 99
Bell peppers
  Garden Bento Boxes:
    Quail Eggs on Frisée
    "Nests," 79
  roasting and peeling, 151
  Silky Tomato Gazpacho, 26
  Spring Asparagus Frittata
    with Peas and Peppers, 113
Bok choy, 22
Botanical Mushroom Tart,
    119–20
Bread. See also Sandwiches
  Garlic Croutons, 69–70
  Toasted Sourdough
    Crostini Topped with
    White Bean Purée and
    Sautéed Greens, 99
Butternut Squash–Apple
    Soup, 39

C

Caesar Salad with Lemon-
    Grilled Chicken, 69–70
Cake, Citrus–Olive Oil, 144
Cantaloupe
  Prawn, Mango, Melon, and
    Cucumber Salad with
    Lemon Vinaigrette, 74–76
Carrots
  Carrot Soup with Chives, 25
  Curried Chicken Pita
    Sandwiches with Carrots
    and Golden Raisins, 102
  Rice Noodle Salad "Nests"
    with Julienned Vegetables
    and Prawns, 56
Champagne Sabayon, 148
Cheese
  Autumn Salad with
    Persimmons and Feta
    Cheese, 87

Botanical Mushroom Tart,
    119–20
Caesar Salad with Lemon-
    Grilled Chicken, 69–70
Crispy Bacon, Arugula,
    Tomato, and Cream
    Cheese Sandwiches, 93
Four-Cheese Pizzas with
    Mixed Herbs and Herb
    Flowers, 110
Fresh Fig and Black Forest
    Ham Sandwiches, 96
Fresh Fig and Crispy
    Prosciutto Salad, 82
Mediterranean Salmon
    Pasta Salad, 73
Mini Pizzas with Italian
    Plum Tomatoes, Red
    Onions, and Basil, 109
Mixed Green Salad with
    Pears, Macadamia Nuts,
    and Brie, 81
Mozzarella, Tomato, and
    Tapenade Sandwiches, 95
Open-Faced Watercress,
    Nasturtium, and
    Cucumber–Cream
    Cheese Sandwiches, 90
Poached Apples
    Stuffed with Brie,
    with Champagne
    Sabayon, 148
Summer Tomato Tarts
    with Goat Cheese and
    Mint, 114
Chicken
  Caesar Salad with Lemon
    Grilled Chicken, 69–70
  Chicken Vegetable Soup
    with Pasta Shells, 35
  Curried Chicken Pita
    Sandwiches with Carrots
    and Golden Raisins, 102

"Dutch Masters" Chicken
    Salad with Red Grapes
    and Toasted Pecans, 52
Fennel, Blood Orange, and
    Grilled Chicken Salad
    with Candied Walnuts, 51
Grilled Chicken Sandwiches
    with Smoked Almonds
    and Dried Apricots, 94
Quinoa Salad with Grilled
    Chicken, Dried Pineapple,
    and Toasted Pistachios, 55
Tahini-Marinated Chicken
    Sandwiches, 103
Chocolate
  Chocolate Chunk Cookies, 133
  Dark Chocolate and Orange
    Pistachio Cookies, 134
Chowder, Summer Squash and
    Fresh Corn, 32
Citrus. See also individual fruits
  Citrus–Olive Oil Cake, 144
  peeling and segmenting, 151
Cookies
  Chocolate Chunk Cookies, 133
  Dark Chocolate and Orange
    Pistachio Cookies, 134
  Sand Dollar Cookies, 137
Corn and Summer Squash
    Chowder, Fresh, 32
Crostini, Toasted Sourdough,
    Topped with White Bean
    Purée and Sautéed Greens, 99
Croutons, Garlic, 69–70
Crumble, Rhubarb-Strawberry, 143
Cucumbers
  Cucumber-Avocado Soup, 29
  Open-Faced Watercress,
    Nasturtium, and
    Cucumber–Cream
    Cheese Sandwiches, 90

Prawn, Mango, Melon, and
    Cucumber Salad with
    Lemon Vinaigrette, 74–76
Rice Noodle Salad "Nests"
    with Julienned Vegetables
    and Prawns, 56
Silky Tomato Gazpacho, 26
Smoked Salmon Sandwiches
    with Radish, Cucumber,
    and Ginger Relish, 100

D
Desserts
    Chocolate Chunk Cookies,
        133
    Citrus–Olive Oil Cake, 144
    Dark Chocolate and Orange
        Pistachio Cookies, 134
    Meyer Lemon Ice, 128
    Poached Apples Stuffed with
        Brie, with Champagne
        Sabayon, 148
    Rhubarb-Strawberry
        Crumble, 143
    Rose Petal Ice Cream, 124
    Sand Dollar Cookies, 137
    Strawberry Tartlets, 138–40
    White Figs with Honey,
        Rum, and Whipped
        Cream, 145
"Dutch Masters" Chicken
    Salad with Red Grapes and
    Toasted Pecans, 52

E
Eggs
    Garden Bento Boxes:
        Quail Eggs on Frisée
        "Nests," 79
    Spring Asparagus Frittata
        with Peas and Peppers, 113

F
Fall garden, 147
Fennel, Blood Orange, and
    Grilled Chicken Salad
    with Candied Walnuts, 51
Figs
    Fresh Fig and Black Forest
        Ham Sandwiches, 96
    Fresh Fig and Crispy
        Prosciutto Salad, 82
    White Figs with Honey,
        Rum, and Whipped
        Cream, 145
Fish. See Salmon
Flowers, 59, 131
    Flower Petal Salad, 61
    Four-Cheese Pizzas with
        Mixed Herbs and Herb
        Flowers, 110
    Open-Faced Watercress,
        Nasturtium, and
        Cucumber–Cream
        Cheese Sandwiches, 90
    Rose Petal Ice Cream, 124
    Rose Petal Syrup, 127
Frisée
    Garden Bento Boxes:
        Quail Eggs on Frisée
        "Nests," 79
    Pan-Seared Sea Scallop
        Salad in Giant Scallop
        Shells with Citrus-Herb
        Vinaigrette, 64
    Prawn, Mango, Melon, and
        Cucumber Salad with
        Lemon Vinaigrette, 74–76
Frittata, Spring Asparagus, with
    Peas and Peppers, 113

G
Garden Bento Boxes: Quail
    Eggs on Frisée "Nests," 79
Gardening
    fall, 147
    spring, 63
    summer, 117
    winter, 43
Garlic
    Garlic Croutons, 69–70
    Rosemary-Garlic Oil, 36
Gazpacho, Silky Tomato, 26
Grapes, Red, "Dutch Masters"
    Chicken Salad with Toasted
    Pecans and, 52
Greens. See also individual greens
    Autumn Salad with Persim-
        mons and Feta Cheese, 87
    Curried Chicken Pita Sand-
        wiches with Carrots and
        Golden Raisins, 102
    "Dutch Masters" Chicken
        Salad with Red Grapes
        and Toasted Pecans, 52
    Garden Bento Boxes: Quail
        Eggs on Frisée "Nests," 79
    Mixed Green Salad with
        Pears, Macadamia Nuts,
        and Brie, 81
    Mixed Greens and Straw-
        berry Salad with Almonds
        and Creamy Orange
        Dressing, 46
    Pan-Seared Sea Scallop
        Salad in Giant Scallop
        Shells with Citrus-Herb
        Vinaigrette, 64
    Quinoa Salad with Grilled
        Chicken, Dried Pineapple,
        and Toasted Pistachios, 55
    Toasted Sourdough
        Crostini Topped with
        White Bean Purée and
        Sautéed Greens, 99

H
Ham
    Fresh Fig and Black Forest
        Ham Sandwiches, 96
    Fresh Fig and Crispy
        Prosciutto Salad, 82
Honey-Ginger Sauce,
    Creamy, 103
Horseradish-Dill Cream Sauce,
    104, 106

I
Ice, Meyer Lemon, 128
Ice Cream, Rose Petal, 124

L
Lemons
    Caesar Salad with Lemon-
        Grilled Chicken, 69–70
    Citrus–Olive Oil Cake, 144
    Creamy Meyer Lemon
        Dressing, 61
    Lemon Vinaigrette, 74, 76
    Meyer Lemon Ice, 128
    Pan-Seared Sea Scallop
        Salad in Giant Scallop
        Shells with Citrus-Herb
        Vinaigrette, 64
    peeling and segmenting, 151
Lettuce, 48
    Caesar Salad with Lemon-
        Grilled Chicken, 69–70
    Fennel, Blood Orange, and
        Grilled Chicken Salad
        with Candied Walnuts, 51
    Flower Petal Salad, 61
    Fresh Fig and Crispy
        Prosciutto Salad, 82
    Mixed Greens and
        Strawberry Salad with
        Almonds and Creamy
        Orange Dressing, 46

Lettuce *continued*
    Rice Noodle Salad "Nests"
      with Julienned Vegetables
      and Prawns, 56
    Smoked Turkey and Romaine
      Salad with Avocado-Lime
      Dressing, 85
Limes
    Avocado-Lime Dressing, 85
    peeling and segmenting, 151

M

Macadamia Nuts, Mixed
    Green Salad with Pears,
    Brie, and, 81
Mango, Prawn, Melon, and
    Cucumber Salad with
    Lemon Vinaigrette, 74–76
Mediterranean Salmon Pasta
    Salad, 73
Meyer lemons
    Creamy Meyer Lemon
      Dressing, 61
    Meyer Lemon Ice, 128
Minestrone with Rosemary-
    Garlic Oil, 36
Mint, 22
    Fresh Pea Soup with Mint
      and Crème Fraîche, 21
    Summer Tomato Tarts
      with Goat Cheese and
      Mint, 114
Mozzarella, Tomato, and
    Tapenade Sandwiches, 95
Mushrooms
    Botanical Mushroom Tart,
      119–20
    Creamy Mushroom Soup
      Topped with Sautéed
      Shiitakes, 40
    Minestrone with Rosemary-
      Garlic Oil, 36

N

Noodles. *See* Pasta and noodles
Nuts, toasting, 151. *See also*
    individual nuts

O

Oil, Rosemary-Garlic, 36
Olives
    Garden Bento Boxes: Quail
      Eggs on Frisée "Nests," 79
    Mediterranean Salmon Pasta
      Salad, 73
    Mozzarella, Tomato, and
      Tapenade Sandwiches, 95
    Tapenade, 95
Oranges
    Citrus–Olive Oil Cake, 144
    Creamy Orange Dressing, 46
    Dark Chocolate and Orange
      Pistachio Cookies, 134
    Fennel, Blood Orange, and
      Grilled Chicken Salad
      with Candied Walnuts, 51
    Orange Champagne
      Vinaigrette, 51
    Orange Champagne
      Vinegar, 150
    peeling and segmenting, 151

P

Pasta and noodles
    Chicken Vegetable Soup
      with Pasta Shells, 35
    Mediterranean Salmon Pasta
      Salad, 73
    Rice Noodle Salad "Nests"
      with Julienned Vegetables
      and Prawns, 56
    Zucchini Blossom Soup, 31
Pears, Mixed Green Salad
    with Macadamia Nuts, Brie,
    and, 81
Peas, 22
    Fresh Pea Soup with Mint
      and Crème Fraîche, 21
    Spring Asparagus Frittata
      with Peas and Peppers, 113
Pecans
    "Dutch Masters" Chicken
      Salad with Red Grapes
      and Toasted Pecans, 52
    toasting, 151

Persimmons, Autumn Salad
    with Feta Cheese and, 87
Pineapple, Dried, Quinoa
    Salad with Grilled Chicken,
    Toasted Pistachios, and, 55
Pistachios
    Dark Chocolate and Orange
      Pistachio Cookies, 134
    Quinoa Salad with Grilled
      Chicken, Dried Pineapple,
      and Toasted Pistachios, 55
    toasting, 151
Pizzas
    Four-Cheese Pizzas with
      Mixed Herbs and Herb
      Flowers, 110
    Mini Pizzas with Italian
      Plum Tomatoes, Red
      Onions, and Basil, 109
    Pizza Dough, 109
Prawns
    Garden Bento Boxes:
      Quail Eggs on Frisée
      "Nests," 79
    poaching and cleaning, 152
    Prawn, Mango, Melon, and
      Cucumber Salad with
      Lemon Vinaigrette, 74–76
    Rice Noodle Salad "Nests"
      with Julienned Vegetables
      and Prawns, 56
Prosciutto, Crispy, and Fresh
    Fig Salad, 82

Q

Quail Eggs on Frisée
    "Nests," 79
Quinoa Salad with Grilled
    Chicken, Dried Pineapple,
    and Toasted Pistachios, 55

R

Radishes
    Flower Petal Salad, 61
    Garden Bento Boxes:
      Quail Eggs on Frisée
      "Nests," 79

Smoked Salmon Sandwiches
    with Radish, Cucumber,
    and Ginger Relish, 100
Raisins, Golden, Curried
    Chicken Pita Sandwiches
    with Carrots and, 102
Rhubarb-Strawberry Crumble, 143
Rice Noodle Salad "Nests"
    with Julienned Vegetables
    and Prawns, 56
Rosemary-Garlic Oil, 36
Roses
    Rose Petal Ice Cream, 124
    Rose Petal Syrup, 127

S

Sabayon, Champagne, 148
Salad dressings
    Avocado-Lime Dressing, 85
    Caesar Dressing, 69–70
    Creamy Meyer Lemon
      Dressing, 61
    Creamy Orange Dressing, 46
    Lemon Vinaigrette, 74, 76
    Orange Champagne
      Vinaigrette, 51
Salads
    Autumn Salad with
      Persimmons and Feta
      Cheese, 87
    Caesar Salad with Lemon-
      Grilled Chicken, 69–70
    "Dutch Masters" Chicken
      Salad with Red Grapes
      and Toasted Pecans, 52
    Fennel, Blood Orange, and
      Grilled Chicken Salad
      with Candied Walnuts, 51
    Flower Petal Salad, 61
    Fresh Fig and Crispy
      Prosciutto Salad, 82
    Garden Bento Boxes: Quail
      Eggs on Frisée "Nests," 79
    Mediterranean Salmon Pasta
      Salad, 73

Mixed Green Salad with
Pears, Macadamia Nuts,
and Brie, 81
Mixed Greens and
Strawberry Salad with
Almonds and Creamy
Orange Dressing, 46
Pan-Seared Sea Scallop
Salad in Giant Scallop
Shells with Citrus-Herb
Vinaigrette, 64
Prawn, Mango, Melon, and
Cucumber Salad with
Lemon Vinaigrette, 74–76
Quinoa Salad with Grilled
Chicken, Dried Pineapple,
and Toasted Pistachios, 55
Rice Noodle Salad "Nests"
with Julienned Vegetables
and Prawns, 56
Smoked Turkey and Romaine
Salad with Avocado-Lime
Dressing, 85
Salmon
Home-Cured Salmon with
Horseradish-Dill Cream
Sauce, 104–6
Mediterranean Salmon Pasta
Salad, 73
Smoked Salmon Sandwiches
with Radish, Cucumber,
and Ginger Relish, 100
Sand Dollar Cookies, 137
Sandwiches
Crispy Bacon, Arugula,
Tomato, and Cream
Cheese Sandwiches, 93
Curried Chicken Pita Sand-
wiches with Carrots and
Golden Raisins, 102
Fresh Fig and Black Forest
Ham Sandwiches, 96
Grilled Chicken Sandwiches
with Smoked Almonds
and Dried Apricots, 94
Mozzarella, Tomato, and
Tapenade Sandwiches, 95

Open-Faced Watercress,
Nasturtium, and
Cucumber–Cream
Cheese Sandwiches, 90
Smoked Salmon Sandwiches
with Radish, Cucumber,
and Ginger Relish, 100
Tahini-Marinated Chicken
Sandwiches, 103
Toasted Sourdough
Crostini Topped with
White Bean Purée and
Sautéed Greens, 99
Sauces
Champagne Sabayon, 148
Creamy Honey-Ginger
Sauce, 103
Horseradish-Dill Cream
Sauce, 104, 106
Scallop Salad, Pan-Seared Sea,
in Giant Scallop Shells with
Citrus-Herb Vinaigrette, 64
Seashells, painting, 66–67
Soups
Butternut Squash–Apple
Soup, 39
Carrot Soup with Chives, 25
Chicken Vegetable Soup
with Pasta Shells, 35
Creamy Mushroom Soup
Topped with Sautéed
Shiitakes, 40
Cucumber-Avocado Soup, 29
Fresh Pea Soup with Mint
and Crème Fraîche, 21
Minestrone with Rosemary-
Garlic Oil, 36
Silky Tomato Gazpacho, 26
Summer Squash and Fresh
Corn Chowder, 32
Zucchini Blossom Soup, 31
Spring garden, 63
Squash. See also Zucchini
Butternut Squash–Apple
Soup, 39
Summer Squash and Fresh
Corn Chowder, 32

Strawberries, 48
Mixed Greens and
Strawberry Salad with
Almonds and Creamy
Orange Dressing, 46
Rhubarb-Strawberry
Crumble, 143
Strawberry Tartlets, 138–40
Summer garden, 117
Swiss chard
Minestrone with Rosemary-
Garlic Oil, 36
Syrup, Rose Petal, 127

T
Tahini-Marinated Chicken
Sandwiches, 103
Tapenade, 95
Tarts and tartlets
Botanical Mushroom Tart,
119–20
Strawberry Tartlets, 138–40
Summer Tomato Tarts
with Goat Cheese and
Mint, 114
Tomatoes
Chicken Vegetable Soup
with Pasta Shells, 35
Crispy Bacon, Arugula,
Tomato, and Cream
Cheese Sandwiches, 93
Garden Bento Boxes:
Quail Eggs on Frisée
"Nests," 79
Mediterranean Salmon
Pasta Salad, 73
Minestrone with Rosemary-
Garlic Oil, 36
Mini Pizzas with Italian
Plum Tomatoes, Red
Onions, and Basil, 109
Mozzarella, Tomato, and
Tapenade Sandwiches, 95
peeling and seeding, 151
Prawn, Mango, Melon, and
Cucumber Salad with
Lemon Vinaigrette, 74–76

Silky Tomato Gazpacho, 26
Summer Tomato Tarts
with Goat Cheese and
Mint, 114
Turkey, Smoked, and Romaine
Salad with Avocado-Lime
Dressing, 85

V
Vinegar, Orange Champagne,
150

W
Walnuts
Candied Walnuts, 152
Chocolate Chunk
Cookies, 133
Fennel, Blood Orange, and
Grilled Chicken Salad
with Candied Walnuts, 51
toasting, 151
Watercress, Nasturtium, and
Cucumber–Cream Cheese
Sandwiches, Open-Faced, 90
Winter garden, 43

Z
Zucchini
Chicken Vegetable Soup
with Pasta Shells, 35
Minestrone with Rosemary-
Garlic Oil, 36
Zucchini Blossom Soup, 31